Routledge Revivals

Local Government Economics in Theory and Practice

First published in 1992, *Local Government Economics in Theory and Practice* is an effort to rectify the lack of a comparative analysis between democratic local governments of various countries and their methods of financing. A series of chapters examines the theoretical basis for different systems of local government finance and how these systems work out in practice. The book covers various aspects of reforms in the United Kingdom and elsewhere, and includes a discussion of the rationale for the community charge. This collection of essays will be of importance to students of economics and public policy.

Local Government Economics in Theory and Practice

Edited by David King

Routledge
Taylor & Francis Group

First published in 1992
by Routledge

This edition first published in 2022 by Routledge
2 Park Square, Milton Park, Abingdon, Oxon, OX14 4RN

and by Routledge
605 Third Avenue, New York, NY 10017

Routledge is an imprint of the Taylor & Francis Group, an informa business

Publisher's Note
The publisher has gone to great lengths to ensure the quality of this reprint but points out that some imperfections in the original copies may be apparent.

Disclaimer
The publisher has made every effort to trace copyright holders and welcomes correspondence from those they have been unable to contact.

A Library of Congress record exists under ISBN: 0415062209

ISBN: 978-1-032-22256-1 (hbk)
ISBN: 978-1-003-27181-9 (ebk)
ISBN: 978-1-032-22257-8 (pbk)

Book DOI 10.4324/9781003271819

Local government economics in theory and practice

Edited by
David King

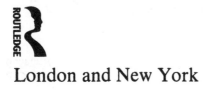

London and New York

First published 1992
by Routledge
11 New Fetter Lane, London EC4P 4EE

Simultaneously published in the USA and Canada
by Routledge
a division of Routledge, Chapman and Hall, Inc.
29 West 35th Street, New York, NY 10001

Typeset by Selectmove
Printed and bound in Great Britain by
Mackays of Chatham PLC, Kent

British Library Cataloguing in Publication Data
Local government economics in theory and practice.
I. King, David N. (David Neden), 1945– 352.041

ISBN 0–415–06220–9

Library of Congress Cataloging in Publication Data
Local government economics in theory and practice/edited by David N. King
Papers presented at a conference held in Ferrara, Italy in 1988, and organized by the Inter-University Centre for the Study of Regional and Local Finance.
Includes bibliographical references and index.
ISBN 0–415–06220–9
1. Local finance–Congresses. 2. Local finance–Europe–Congresses. I. King, David, 1945– . II. Inter-University Centre for the Study of Regional and Local Finance.
HJ9105.L62 1992
336′.014–dc20

91–24979
CIP

Contents

Figures

Tables

Contributors

Robert Bennett: London School of Economics, England

Glen Bramley: University of Bristol, England

Antoni Castells: University of Barcelona, Spain

Gianluigi Galeotti: University of Perugia, Italy

Gordon Hamilton: Cheshire County Council, England

David King: University of Stirling, Scotland

Julian Le Grand: University of Bristol, England

William Low: Brunel University, London, England

Françoise Navarre: University of Paris, France

Jeffrey Owens: OECD, Paris, France

Stefano Piperno: University of Turin, Italy

Giancarlo Pola: University of Ferrara, Italy

Remy Prud'homme: University of Paris, France

Walter Santagata: University of Turin, Italy

John Sellgren: London School of Economics, England

Joaquim Sole-Vilanova: University of Barcelona, Spain

Eric Thöni: University of Innsbruck, Austria

Horst Zimmermann: Philipps University, Marburg, Germany

Acknowledgement

The editor is most grateful to Miss Jackie Wright for her care in typing the papers in this book.

Introduction

Giancarlo Pola and David King

All the countries of western Europe have some form of democratic local government. Thus all of these countries have to consider what is the appropriate role for local authorities and how those authorities should be financed. These have been active issues in many countries in recent years, yet there has been little effort by economists from different countries to meet and see what they can learn from each other.

In an attempt to promote an international sharing of ideas, a conference was organised in 1988 by CIFREL (the Inter-University Centre for the Study of Regional and Local Finance). The conference took place in Ferrara, Italy, and the papers in this book were first presented there. It is our hope and belief that they will be of interest to anyone with an interest in local finance.

Gianluigi Galeotti's paper develops a public choice approach to the need for decentralisation. It envisages a world where parties play a subtle game of rent-seeking, the ingredients of which are political information, ideology and voters in search of their maximum welfare. Given such a setting, Galeotti comes to the conclusion (which is not far from the famous neo-classical theorem given by Wallace Oates) that public decisions in less centralised systems reflect citizens' opinions more and politicians' wishes less than in centralised systems.

Erich Thöni's approach to fiscal federalism underlines the need for not confining the discussion to a purely 'economic' theory: he goes back to the perhaps old-fashioned but solid concept of 'political economy'. Such an approach – Thöni says – has first of all to incorporate the political dimensions of federalism and has therefore to be built on both politics and economics. This means analysing the relationship between the institutional arrangements and the economic policies of state and local authorities. Analysing the 'politics' of federal government means studying the decision-making processes which lead to the outcomes; analysing the 'economics' of it means mainly concentrating on the outcomes. So, the role of institutions and 'constitutions' in the 'efficiency' of decentralisation is brought out.

Of course, even a purely 'economic' approach to fiscal federalism has much to say, as is shown by a vast literature, mainly of British and American origin. David King's paper discusses some economic reasoning about local government's functions, financing and activity. He covers a wide range of topics including the roles of local authorities as redistributors and law-makers, the role of taxation in financing lower-tier governments, and the 'flypaper effect' of central government grants to local authorities. His paper suggests that standard economic doctrine can lead to fruitful insights into the behaviour of local authorities.

Joaquim Sole-Vilanova and Antoni Castells give further thought to the prospect of using standard economics to analyse issues that arise from the existence of local government. Issues they consider are the incidence of taxes (with special reference to the property tax) on the price of factors; the existence and extent of fiscally-induced migration; the possibility of fiscal competition between jurisdictions; the optimal size of jurisdictions; the equalising capacity of the grant system; and the redistributive effects of local finance and expenditure.

The economic effects of a system of local government obviously depend on the methods of its finance and on the level, kind and nature of its expenditure. Many different methods of finance are now in use. Jeffrey Owens's paper gives a valuable insight into the methods used in OECD countries. Focusing on local taxation as one of the most intriguing questions with regard to local government, Owens considers some of the major questions about local taxes. Which taxes are appropriate for financing local government? What is an appropriate local tax mix? What is the effect of the relative reliance of local government on local taxes and tax-sharing arrangements in promoting local accountability?

The choice of the appropriate local taxes and of the specific form they should take is crucial, especially in countries where local taxes account for several percentage points of GDP. Inevitably, local taxation becomes a major concern to the parties in power. When politicians have 'strong' feelings about the inefficiency or the inequity of existing local taxes, then the results can be a revolutionary change, like replacing a property tax with a 'community charge' as in the United Kingdom. Glen Bramley, Gordon Hamilton and Julian Le

Grand have produced a paper in which they use evidence from Cheshire to challenge the claim made by the Government at the time that the 'community charge' resembles a charge for services, so that tax liabilities relate to the use and benefit derived from services.

Reforms of local taxation systems can be far less drastic than the British substitution of the community charges for the domestic rates, and yet still be as hard and time-consuming to implement. Certainly this seems to be the German experience, according to Horst Zimmermann's paper. In 1969 a reform of local finance took place in Germany, whereby communities became less dependent on the business tax (*Gewerbesteur*) and more dependent on their share of the national income tax. However, as Zimmermann points out, the reform did not abolish the 'inherent weaknesses' of the business tax, and this means that another reform is almost inevitable. Zimmermann considers other possible reforms in local taxation, including the possiblity of allowing local governments to be included in the value added tax sharing scheme.

While relatively underdeveloped in Germany, property taxation at the local level is important in France. There it takes up two basic forms, one related to 'non-developed land' (*impôt foncier non-bati*) and the other to 'developed land' (*impôt foncier bati*). Although property taxation is generally considered a 'good' source of finance for local government, Remy Prud'homme and Francoise Navarre's paper shows that French local communities suffer from quite different fiscal endowments deriving from property taxation. These very large disparities are probably in part due to the small size of French 'communes'; but this is enough, Prud'homme and Navarre suggest, to undermine the idea that French local authorities can realistically choose their own policies and tax and service packages.

By way of contrast, the idea that local governments provide the specific tax and service packages that are demanded by their citizens is taken as a starting point in the 'Turin experiment' referred to by Stefano Piperno and Walter Santagata. This experiment was an attempt to induce a representative sample of inhabitants to reveal their preferences about the way local government manages economic resources. It was carried out through a carefully-designed questionnaire. There did seem to be some correspondence between the size and composition of the budget on the one side, and citizens' demand for public goods, on the other. However, the authors are not convinced that this correspondence proves that local authorities are run by politicians whose sole aim is to maximise the welfare of local voters.

Although the primary tasks of all local governments in the world remain the delivery of services demanded, or needed, by local communities and the raising of the required amounts of money, it is an open question whether and to what extent they might go beyond that and, possibly, cooperate with upper tiers of government to achieve faster economic development. This is an important issue which touches on such questions as wealth creation, employment and the distribution of economic activities. The possible role of British local authorities in development is the subject of the paper by Robert Bennett and John Sellgren. They discuss the conditions under which individual businesses may wish to exercise wider social responsibilities, act collectively with each other, and join with local government economic initiatives. The results suggest that local authorities should not be kept out of the development field.

We hope this book will help a wide audience to understand better some of the problems which are very common to all European countries.

1 Decentralisation and political rents[1]

Gianluigi Galeotti

INTRODUCTION

The economic theory of subcentral government lacks a theory of politics. Decentralisation has been positively analysed and normatively discussed from a variety of points of view, but the relevance of political behaviour has been largely ignored. This paper argues that an analysis of political behaviour is of critical importance. It suggests that an important reason for decentralising the public sector is to reduce politicians' rents, so that all other more traditional concerns can be viewed as somehow instrumental to the improvement of public competition. After a brief consideration of the role played by political parties, the paper presents a model of political rents, tests its validity, and discusses how decentralisation comes to reduce the amount of those rents.

In a rather romantic vein, the literature on decentralisation often assumes that decentralisation enhances citizens' involvement in decision-making, improves grass-roots democracy, and makes the signalling of preferences cheaper. As far as competition is concerned, this is thought to be confined directly to competition between local governments for residents, firms and tax revenues. Though some notice is taken of competition between political parties for electoral support, competition for power between different governments, or levels of government, is considered with suspicion as a danger to a smooth working of the political process.

Tiebout's competition for residents, as well as Oates's theorem (1972), face the problem of reconciling geographical differences in people's tastes with the spatial impact of different public goods. Some authors have challenged the analytical legitimacy of insulating those features from the working of the political process (Breton and Scott, 1978) and have questioned the relevance of the Oates's theorem. However, we are interested here in a more articulated discussion of the positive features of public decision-making. For the sake of our argument, suppose that individuals' preferences are homogeneously distributed with high costs of mobility and that there are no spatial limits to public goods; then ask whether there are still reasons for decentralising the public structure among different levels of governments. Without discussing possible replies within the conventional welfare approach, we intend to show (in a spirit close to the analysis of Dahl and Tufte, 1973) that decentralisation still has an important role to play: that of reducing politicians' rents.

The bulk of our argument can be summarised easily. We start with the observation that politicians and political parties do much more than reflect the views of their supporters. They shape those views in the process of weighing popular approval against the perceived value of proposed policies to politicians themselves. Centralisation affects that balance by requiring greater commitment by voters towards their political parties and by allowing greater scope for interaction between politicans, an interaction which tends to benefit politicans at the expense of voters. If institutional design and political competition affect the degrees of politicans' freedom – their 'rents' – then public decisions in less centralised countries reflect citizens' opinions more and politicians' wishes less than do centralised systems (Galeotti, 1987).

In what follows, we first consider briefly the role played by political parties in guaranteeing the vertical and horizontal links that make possible the working of representative democracy. (Vertical links are those between citizens and politicians, while horizontal links are those between politicians.) Then we show how decentralisation could affect the relative development of those links, and we establish a simple relationship between political rents and decentralisation. The paper concludes by suggesting how the propositions it makes could be tested empirically.

THE ROLE OF POLITICAL PARTIES

'One of the main characteristics of the economic theory of subcentral government is that, as a rule, it lacks a theory of politics' (Salmon, 1987). To fill this void it is necessary to clarify the role played by a political party in the working of a representative democracy. We can do this by seeing its role as being one of offering a political 'exchange' in which some citizens will pledge their political support (by way of votes, donations, canvassing and other activities) in exchange for a representation of their political 'opinions'. It should be noted that we are not referring to the representation by political parties of well-defined individual preferences, but to the representation of 'opinions', or what J. S. Mill (1863) regarded as general points of view about what the object of present or future public decisions should be. (Galeotti and Breton, 1986, discuss the benefits of political exchanges to voters.)

The exchanges noted in the last paragraph have very precarious foundations, or bases, because the relationships between parties and voters are not self-enforcing (Telser, 1980) and are not supported by 'legal guarantees'. Remember that votes cannot be sold or revoked, that representatives need support only at election times and that representatives have to make decisions on all the issues that may emerge during the course of their term of office. Now the absence of a legal framework and the vagueness of the relationship between voters and representatives make it extremely hard for voters or representatives to control each other, and this problem is exacerbated by the tendency of politicians to be opportunist and the tendency for voters' preferences to be volatile.

We therefore submit that if, in spite of all these difficulties, the democratic system does not actually collapse, then this must be as a result of the guarantees and the support that are supplied by political parties. Because any party is concerned about its long-term survival, it is motivated to control closely the behaviour of its representatives, and it is also motivated to use many devices to stimulate support from voters; these devices include items such as rallies, canvassing, debates and public meetings. Thus a party tries to create a favourable relationship with its voters. It can be seen as trying to secure a 'trust' with the voters (Breton and Wintrobe, 1982) or as investing in an effort to secure a 'reputation' (Shapiro, 1983). It is these activities of political parties that ensure that the democratic system works.

VERTICAL AND HORIZONTAL EXCHANGES

The effect of political parties in generating support is given empirical confirmation by the differing levels of turn-out found in elections where the influences of parties is different. Think of the low turn-out in referendums (Galeotti and Breton, 1986), or of what happens in those United States' local elections where the presence of political parties is precluded. As Lee (1963) showed, turn-out is typically lower in non-partisan elections than in partisan elections.

A political party, however, while acting as guarantor of the 'vertical' relationship between voters and representatives, also makes possible the development of 'horizontal' relationships, such as those between ordinary elected representatives and between them and party leaders. These horizontal exchanges help political activity to take place by facilitating the initiatives, agreements, fights and compromises that are everyday news. Now although the horizontal relationships are necessary for political action to take place, it must be stressed that the balance between vertical and horizontal relationships can be taken to characterise different political systems. It can be demonstrated that a system in which horizontal exchanges prevail over vertical ones leads to different results from those obtainable where instead the reverse occurs (Breton and Galeotti, 1985).

We must now discuss the impact that decentralisation has on the institutional elements that influence the relative development of the two types of exchanges.

DECENTRALISATION AND POLITICAL BEHAVIOUR

Let us begin by considering vertical exchanges. The assumption of political exchanges based on the representations of broad opinions rather than specific preferences implies that when the number of functions of a certain level of government increases, then the appeal to opinions becomes more important and thus the role of political parties becomes more crucial. However, voters face the problem that the more vague the principles of a political party become, the more costly it is to see exactly what these principles are and to see how they might be affected by the compromises and adjustments that characterise political activity. If the precariousness of vertical relationships increases, then the activities carried out by a party are likely to strengthen its ties with the voters. This is a testable hypothesis which would not be put forward by those who ignore the role performed by political parties.

For the moment, however, let us consider another effect. A greater voter commitment towards political parties allows the development of stronger horizontal political ties. The discussion can be summarised in the following terms. As the centralisation of the public sector increases, so the link between politicians and their supporters tends to become stronger. But as the costs to voters of working out the views of different parties rise, so voters are likely to change their allegiances less often. This means that politicians' degree of freedom in interpreting and applying the party ideology to everyday policy issues increases. If we regard ideology as a political opinion strictly controlled by the party apparatus, then it could be inferred that the centralisation of political decisions favours the 'ideologisation' of political platforms. As a final step, if we can relate this ideologisation of party platforms to the much lower oscillation of electoral results occuring in centralised politics, then we could face a kind of inversion of the logic of representative democracy: it is no longer the citizens who signal their preferences to politicians, but the latter – the guarantors of the ideology – who indicate to the former what they must 'prefer' to remain faithful to the party line.

The result which we wish to emphasise is that with the centralisation of the public sector, horizontal exchanges increase and thus the degree of freedom enjoyed by politicians in managing the daily articulation of political choices also increases. It now remains to establish how those degrees of freedom can be interpreted in terms of 'political rents', which are defined as an excess of votes over their opportunity costs.

THE FEATURES OF 'POLITICAL PRODUCTS'

First, let us show that, in political markets, as in economic markets, political rents depend on the elasticity of demand. To do this, we have to define the characteristics of the 'product' that is pursued by voters and see how the elasticity of political demand decreases as centralisation increases.

As for the 'political product', let us suppose that voters' appreciation of the representation of opinions by a party has a further feature, that of *efficacy*, as revealed in terms of a party's electoral strength and its ability to influence political outcomes. In other words, to the Millian dimension previously discussed, we add a second dimension that somehow takes into account Stigler's observation (1972), according to which voters are interested in the effectiveness of their vote. The latter feature permits us to integrate the traditional spatial analysis of choices with a further dimension that differentiates the 'products' offered by parties that belong to the same 'ideological area'. This is very helpful in interpreting what happens in the context of multi-party political situations.

In this way we can distinguish two different and convergent sources of rents: one derives from the demand for ideology (that is to say the representation of broad opinion), while the other derives from the demand for 'effective' political parties. Before showing how decentralisation implies a more elastic political demand, let us stress that voters have different information costs in trying to gauge the efficacy of a party in terms of its electoral strength and its political initiative. While it is relatively easy – even for the less informed voter – to know the electoral strength of a party as revealed by its past electoral results, the evaluation of its political initiatives is more complex.

Because of this assymetry, it is plausible to suggest that electorally stronger parties (that is to say those parties directly competing for government) enjoy a relative advantage. Among the voters interested in the political efficacy of their vote, those who lack adequate information will tend to rely more heavily on electoral strength as a signal of efficacy. The empirical support of this contention is discussed in Galeotti (1988), where it is shown that when voting is compulsory, two major parties systematically obtain more votes. The explanation suggested there is based on information costs: among voters compelled to vote, those who would have preferred to stay at home for lack of information find it simpler to limit their choice to the two parties that are expected to be electorally strongest. In Dutch post-war elections, for example, when the obligation to vote was relaxed at the end of the 1960s, the total vote of the two major parties decreased from 54 per cent to 46 per cent, while minor parties lost altogether only one percentage point.

Incidentally, it is likely that those voters who are interested in efficacy will be more sensitive to political information than those who vote on an ideological basis. At the same time, it is precisely this greater sensitivity that pushes political parties to greater initiatives, inducing them to dedicate themselves to something that, for lack of a better word, we shall define as 'political attention'. With this, we intend to refer to party initiatives such as mobilisation, getting attention in the media, and contractual efforts made inside or outside political coalitions. For political parties, this 'attention' dedicated to the need for support by voters is an activity that soaks up resources, but at the same time is the principal variable that they are able to control, at least in the short term.

AN INTERPRETATION OF POLITICAL RENTS

On the basis of what has been suggested so far, it is possible to present in Figure 1.1 a simple graphic representation of political rents. These rents are measured in terms of the excess votes that a party obtains; this excess is the difference between the total number of votes a party actually receives – its total 'revenue' of votes – and the 'cost' of obtaining these votes. The 'cost' is defined as the votes it forgoes by diverting its efforts away from groups of potential voters who might have supported it to the groups it actually did seek to persuade to vote for it. It is only in the presence of this excess of votes that a party can enjoy the freedom to pursue objectives at variance with those desired or expected by its voters. Moreover, its degree of freedom is a function of the excess.

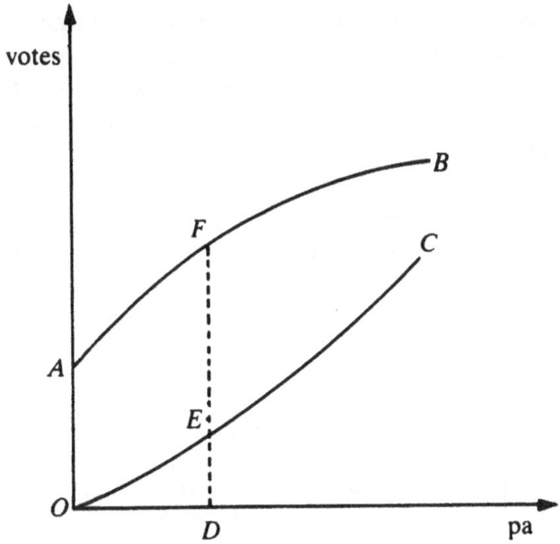

Figure 1.1 Correlation of votes and political attention

In Figure 1.1 we measure votes on the y-axis and 'political attention' (*pa*) on the x-axis. This 'attention' presents an opportunity cost by absorbing resources that could be utilised in different ways, for example making initiatives to other social groups. If one accepts this interpretation, then the *OC* curve can be seen as an expression of votes lost, that is, of the votes that the party in question could have won had it made initiatives to other social groups. This is an interpretation consistent with Schumpeter's observation regarding the ability of 'political managers' to transform latent wants of people into political factors. In our case this is equivalent to the ability to select the combination of wants and social groups for which the difference between costs and gains – both measured in terms of votes – is greater.

On the demand side, the preceding analysis suggests that there may be a fixed component, shown by *OA*, and a variable component, shown by *AB*. The 'fixed' votes shown by *OA* are those of voters who are chiefly interested in the political opinions of the party. The 'variable' votes shown by *OB* are those of voters who are chiefly interested in the efficacy of the party. Remember that voters can measure the efficacy of parties, and to persuade voters that it will be efficacious a party has to devote resources to attracting attention and making political initiative.

The party will opt for the position where marginal 'cost' (which is considered to increase at an increasing rate) equals marginal 'revenue'. Thus it will settle on the amount of political attention shown by *OD*, and it will receive a 'rent' equal to *EF* which is, of course, measured in votes. The crucial point to grasp here is the connection between rents and the elasticity of political demand. Political parties would enjoy a maximum of freedom in pursuing their own objectives – by completely ignoring the needs of voters – if the demand for their party (that is the willingness to vote for it) was completely fixed; for then *AB* would be horizontal and the highest attainable rent would be found with a zero expenditure on political attention.

POLITICAL RENTS AND DECENTRALISATION

We are now able to sum up our reasoning and reach conclusions that can be empirically verified. We started with the proposition that the links between voters and representatives would become stronger, and thus the role played by the more important political parties would become stronger, as the degree of centralisation of the public sector increased. Graphically, this suggests that the fixed components *OA* faced by a party will become greater as the functions given to the level of government with which it is concerned increase. More precisely, if we apply this proposition to a context such as the Italian one, we must expect that the links between voters and parties will become stronger (and thus *OA* will become higher) as we pass from local elections (which concern few public functions) to national elections. It follows that if we are willing to measure the strength of this link approximately in terms of voting participation, then we should expect an increase in turn-out as we go from local to national elections. That this is a far from obvious conclusion is shown by the fact that it is the opposite to that deducible from economic interpretations of political behaviour that neglect the role played by political parties. (In fact, if one follows Schumpeter (1942), who suggests that citizens understand best those problems with which they have a more direct experience, or Downs (1957), who argues that the relevance of an individual's vote must decrease with the increased size of the electoral body, one would expect abstentions to increase as we move from local to national elections.)

Empirical data, however, are consistent with our interpretation since, from local to national elections, turn-out ratios systematically increase in practically all countries. According to data discussed in Galeotti (1987) this was the case in all countries for which post-1945 information was available, except for Japan. Indeed in Sweden, voters' participation for the central government elections was as much as 18 per cent higher than it was for local elections. (Analogous observations have been formulated by Tingsten (1963) for the pre-war period.)

As regards Italy, the first column of Table 1.1 shows the same tendency in some regions which have been chosen to exemplify the point. Though the difference in the participation rate between the two levels is not conspicuous, it is significant, especially if one considers the strong 'political' significance that is always attributed to local elections by the incumbent government.

Table 1.1 Aggregate percentage results in some Italian local and national elections (average of elections held in the period 1960–78)

Constituency	*Abstentions*		*Major parties*[1]		*Minor parties*	
	Local	*National*	*Local*	*National*	*Local*	*National*
Liguria	10.81	8.54	56.61	60.28	32.57	31.17
Marche	10.44	8.04	60.43	66.97	29.13	24.99
Umbria (+ Rieti)	10.40	7.89	58.47	66.21	31.08	25.90
Lazio (− Rieti)	11.14	8.07	53.82	58.43	35.04	33.50
Basilicata	15.89	15.39	58.28	63.11	25.83	21.50

Source: Elaboration of data from: *Results of Administrative and Political Elections* (Rome: ISTAT), various years

Note: 1 Sum of the votes of the Christian Democratic Party and the Communist Party

We can now generalise this result, suggesting that if the existing link between parties and voters tends to diminish if the functions given to a certain level of government decrease, then the rents which are due to the constant component (*OA* in Figure 1.1) should also diminish.

As regards the variable component (*AB*), we hypothesise that the slope of *AB* tends to diminish just the same as we go from senior to junior levels of government. This is because voters are likely to be better informed about different parties at the local level – and are much less likely to be persuaded to switch from one party to another as a result of 'political attention' spending. Consequently, it will be expected that the major parties would receive less votes in local than in national elections. This is an admittedly loose implication, but it is one that is confirmed by the figures shown in Table 1.1. The lower rate of participation in local elections not only works to the disadvantage of the major parties, but they in turn then lose to the advantage of the minor parties. (It might, perhaps, be argued that the political opinions expressed by minor parties are more relevant at the local level, but this seems implausible.) In other words, whether the lower support that the major parties receive at the local level translates into votes for the minor parties (almost completely, as in Basilicata) or into a low overall turn-out (as in Lazio and Liguria), we are always in the presence of a tendency consistent with the hypothesis of a decrease of political rents enjoyed by the major parties at the local level.

CONCLUDING REMARKS

The choice of a government and the representation of opinions are two fundamental functions performed by elections at all levels of government. But the degree of freedom that politicians enjoy depends on how centralised or decentralised the public sector is. To develop this proposition, we have considered the role carried out by a political party in making possible the working of representative democracy. The decentralisation of the public sector influences this role, promoting a greater development of vertical relationships (between voters and representatives) rather than horizontal ones (among politicians). This happens to be so because with decentralisation the elasticity of the political demand faced by political parties increases, as indirectly confirmed by empirical evidence.

NOTES

1 The author thanks the participants in the Seminar and in particular Mssrs Battiato, Brosio, Dafflon, Pommerehne and Stefani for their comments.

REFERENCES

Breton, A. and Scott, A. (1978) *The Economic Constitution of Federal States*, Toronto: Toronto University Press.

Breton, A. and Galeotti, G. (1985) 'Is proportional representation always the best electoral rule?', *Public Finance – Finances Publiques* 30:1.

Breton, A. and Wintrobe, R. (1986) *The Logic of Bureaucratic Conduct*, Cambridge: Cambridge University Press.

Dahl, R. and Tufte, E. (1973) *Size and Democracy*, Stanford: Stanford University Press.

Downs, A. (1957) *An Economic Theory of Democracy*, New York: Harper & Row.

Galeotti, G. (1987) 'Political exchanges and decentralisation', *European Journal of Political Economy* 3:1.

——(1988) 'Does an increase in the number of political parties improve political competition?', unpublished paper.

Galeotti, G. and Breton, A. (1986) 'An economic theory of political parties', *Kyklos* 39:1.

Lee, E.C. (1960) *The Politics of Nonpartisanship: A Study of California City Elections*, Berkeley: University of California Press.

Mill, J.S. (1863), *Considerations on Representative Government*, New York: Bobbs-Merrill, 1958.

Oates, W.E. (1972) *Fiscal Federalism*, New York: Harcourt, Brace, Jovanovich.

Salmon, P. (1987) 'Decentralisation as an incentive scheme', *Oxford Review of Economic Policy* 3:1.

Sandmo, A. (1970) 'The effect of uncertainty on saving decisions', *Review of Economic Studies* 37:3.

Schumpeter, J.A. (1943) *Capitalism, Socialism and Democracy*, London: Allen & Unwin, 1976.

Shapiro, C., (1983) 'Premiums for high quality products as returns to reputation', *Quarterly Journal of Economics* 98:4.

Stigler, G.J. (1972) 'Economic competition and political Competition', *Public Choice* 13: Fall.

Telser, L.G. (1980) 'A theory of self-enforcing agreements' *Journal of Business* 53:1.

Tingsten, H. (1963) *Political Behaviour: Studies in Election Statistics*, Ottowa: Bedminster Press.

2 The political economy of tax and expenditure decentralisation

Are there answers for constitutional reform?

Erich Thöni

INTRODUCTION

Economic analyses of 'federalism', defined in the usual economists' sense, or of 'decentralisation', which will be used synonymously in this paper, have concentrated over time on two main issues (Hamlin, 1985). First, does the existence of a federal or decentralised form of government pose new questions to the science of public finance and, if it does, how can these questions be answered within the structure of that science? Secondly, does federalism matter, and under what circumstances will a federal structure be desirable?

The first issue raises problems of policy design within a federal state, and has led to an extensive literature on financial questions. The second issue concentrates on federalism as a decision-making process, and on different aspects of and different approaches to 'optimal' federal structures (e.g. Kirsch, 1977).

As Quigley and Rubinfeld (1986) point out,

> the state–local public finance literature of the 1960s was marked generally by an emphasis on the advantages of the federal government as a raiser of revenue and as a corrective mechanism for market failures at the state and local levels. The state–local public finance literature of the 1980s is marked, in contrast, by sceptism about the ability of the federal government to perform these functions, and also by a renewed emphasis on the presumed allocative efficiency arising from a system of multiple governments in which voting with one's feet is a serious option.

Why has this scepticism arisen? Is this renewed emphasis legitimate?

The conclusion of this paper coincides partly with the main argument of Wiseman (1987) in his long survey and appraisal of the political economy of federalism 'that it is difficult to derive policy-relevant normative propositions about federal financial relations'. To this it is appropriate to add that there is still a lot of work to be done to understand political decisions and to relate them to the standard fiscal federalism literature.

The sections which follow summarise some of the main lines of argument in the so-called 'pure' economic theory of federalism, pointing to the essential decision-making politics within federalism. Some of the recent arguments in the literature which show new possibilities for a 'politico-economic' theory of federalism are dealt with, and finally the present general state of theory is summarised.

THE PURE ECONOMIC THEORY OF FEDERALISM: 'FISCAL FEDERALISM'

Following Hamlin (1985) it is possible to avoid an extensive review of the enormous literature (which is discussed by Bolutoglu, 1976), by saying that the fiscal federalist approach is distinguished by two major characteristics. First, it maintains that there is an important distinction between economic and political federalism. Second, it maintains that the optimal size of area for each type of public policy can generally be determined as a result of a calculus based on the spatial, technical and cost conditions; if the optimal size for each type of policy cannot be determined through a calculus, then competition between governments of the same level might lead to the optimal structure.

The first characteristic assumes that decision-making bodies are independent, and thus it discusses regional variations in policies only in terms of varying circumstances or preferences. The second characteristic maintains that the optimal degree of decentralisation for any activity can be calculated on a pure cost-benefit analysis. It may initially suggest that there should be as many tiers of government as there are functions, but on a deeper analysis of costs usually suggests fewer tiers.

With regard to the behaviour of governments, the Pigovian approach of diminishing marginal utility is often used – governments behave like individuals. Their concern is to relate the benefits of their expenditures to their costs. The competition approach based on Tiebout (1956) is rather different. It offered the first 'process-orientated' approach to constitutional questions. It assumes that jurisdictions already exist and have been given certain functions, and it maintains that citizens compare the benefits received from public services with their cost. Then they move to those jurisdictions that suit them best. Therefore, people of similar 'fiscal' tastes move together and in doing this they produce an (approximately) 'optimum spatial pattern'. This approach tends to neglect any discussion of how to establish the competition.

In embodying these characteristics, the mainstream version of fiscal federalism fails to develop any really practical arguments concerning decentralisation. It appears that there is a divergence between normative economic principle, on the one hand, and the preferences of politician actors on the other (Weingast *et al.*, 1981). The analyses either start with the assumption that first of all there are no public authorities at all, and then postulate a structure of federalism from scratch; or they assume that there is initially no jurisdiction other than a single central government which aims to establish 'real' authorities. The governments are seen as 'perfect' ones, concerned only with the 'public interest' and efficiency. Fiscal federalism therefore has a very naive theory of government.

As Wiseman (1987) shows, the Pigovian approach has to be rejected for the following reasons: it requires acceptance of an organic theory of the state, its policy prescriptions derive from implausible and untestable propositions about the capacities of persons, and the approach can throw no light upon the special fiscal problems of existing federations.

THE POLITICAL ECONOMY OF FEDERALISM

Constitutional federalism is characterised by a formal division of political power. There exists more than one level of government, and these jurisdictions do have at least some guaranteed autonomy to fulfil political functions, to decide upon expenditures and to tax. This can be defined as a decentralised jurisdictional set-up. In contrast, the delegated power within a unitary state can be defined as a deconcentrated set-up (Esterbauer and Thöni, 1981).

Historically, it should be realised that there are few recent examples of constitutions which were designed from scratch. One such was West Germany, but here the set-up was designed by exogenous forces, namely the Allies, and within their discussions non-economic arguments played the dominant role. Contrary to the general idea of strengthening the 'state' through a federal structure, they seemed to envisage a weakening of the 'state', especially the central power, through federalism.

In any constitutional set-up, especially federalism, 'it is not easy to envisage any significant changes in public finance arrangements that do not have implications for such matters as regional autonomy and the separation of powers' (Wiseman, 1987). This holds true even for unitarian structures, where the changes will not affect autonomy in a formal sense, but will affect the deconcentration of power from the central government to local governments.

FROM A 'PURE' TO A 'POLITICAL-ECONOMY' THEORY OF FEDERALISM

Generally speaking, up to the 1970s economic models mostly ignored the governmental set-up completely, or treated it, in Wiseman's words (1987), as a sort of aberration, and this was especially so in fiscal federalism. Fiscal federalism mostly saw federalism as a means to economic ends which should be efficiently reached. In other words, the federal structure was used as an instrument for the implementation of (normative) aims. These aims were mostly secured by an ill-defined 'actor' based on an organic or communitarian paradigm (as Buchanan, 1988, would express it) behaving like an individuum or supra-individuum. The behaviour of the mayor or the median voter was modelled analogously to the behaviour of a consumer in the private economy (Oates, 1972, and Quigley and Rubinfeld, 1986).

In the 1980s the model of a passive optimising decision-maker or median voter came under attack, chiefly because Leviathan was growing. In discussing US tax policy, the case for the deductibility of non-federal taxes was challenged by models which saw local taxes as benefit taxes for publicly-provided goods, and by general equilibrium models of local taxes which saw property taxes as more progressive than income taxes (Quigley and Rubinfeld, 1986).

However, not even these newer approaches offer a coherent, or even a consistent, view of the state–local public economy. They are incapable of providing a useful view or a valuable understanding of the choices and evaluations on which federalism is built, or to put it differently, on the essentials of federalism.

This does not mean that the economic or public choice analyses are irrelevant, but within a decentralised set-up they have to be enriched by realistic federal dimensions. Federal structures are not designed from scratch: they seem much more the outcome of a permanently ongoing change through the decision-making processes on multiple issues. With regard to behaviour, there might be different views on the aims and means to use as inputs into the political decision processes. In addition to very rational, benefit-maximising behaviour there may be some altruistic, or at least citizen-orientated behaviour, which alters the outcomes.

Therefore, the analytical questions have to be changed. Saying this is not only to question the optimal, efficient federal structure, it is more to demand a positive analysis of the behaviour of the relevant individual actors, who include the citizens, the politicians or officeholders, the bureaucrats or government officials, and interest group representatives. It is also necessary to analyse the behaviour of groups of individuals or 'collective actors' such as the central government, the states, local authorities and their organisations, interest groups and political parties (Thöni, 1986, examines these issues). Moreover, it is necessary to ask whether and how all these different actors are transformed into a constitutional structure which is accepted so that the existence of the federal state is not in danger (these questions were recently raised by Kirsch, 1987).

This change of questions has profound effects. No longer is the primary issue the question of the optimal federal structure or the efficient allocative or distributive structure; rather interest is focused on the conditions under which the federal state exists and develops. This approach is based on the ideas of Breton and Scott (1980), who split their analysis of the design of federations into a 'design by machines' (a welfare or outcome-orientated approach) and into a 'design by politicians' (a process-orientated approach).

It seems that a 'political-economy' approach, analysing the process and the outcomes, or, to put it another way, the structure and performance, is in demand. What could be the elements or further questions of such a new political-economy theory of federalism?

Such a theory of federalism has first of all to incorporate the 'political' dimensions of federalism, and has therefore to be built on both politics and economics. It has to analyse the relationships between institutional arrangements and the types of economic policy which are derived from them. In other words it has to integrate the 'processes' of decision making as well as the outcomes of these processes – it has to be process-orientated as well as outcome-orientated.

The first issue which has to be addressed is that of whether to use a normative 'individualistic' or 'organic' approach to analyse the processes. As Buchanan (1988) points out, the rejection of the organic paradigm in favour of an individualistic one has important implications:

> If individuals, or organisations of individuals, are the units that

> enter into exchanges, then the values or interests of individuals are the only values that exist. And, if we adhere strictly to the individualistic benchmark, there can be no fundamental distinction between economics and politics or, more generally, between the economy and the polity.

As Weingast *et al.* (1981) have already shown in their analysis, political institutions transform the economic basis of costs and benefits into political costs and benefits, and it is the latter which define rational decisions for political actors. They conclude that as political institutions fundamentally alter the perceptions and incidence of benefits and costs, so they systematically bias project choices away from the efficient outcomes; and they do so differently at the different levels of government (Thöni, 1986).

Kirsch (1987) shows in his analysis that federalism, and therefore the degree of decentralisation, seems to be the result of an interplay between centrifugal and centripetal forces. Moreover, these centrifugal and centripetal forces are themselves dependent and determined by the federal structure. Centrifugal forces try to minimise 'cleavages' and conflicts within jurisdictions by building up homogeneous jurisdictions; but this in turn tends to build up conflicts between jurisdictions. If these cannot be resolved by negotiations, then centripetal forces will try to overcome the conflicts between jurisdictions by centralisation and, in doing that, may build up other conflicts. Kirsch's analysis stops there, but he points to the fact that all this interplay should be further investigated in empirical studies of federal countries. Preferences for public goods and services in an area are very much dependent on the 'culture' of the area. Factors such as language, religion, race and history do matter, and provide a good argument for decentralisation.

In general, there are dramatic differences in the optimal scale of government for different functions. Olson (1986) considers the economies of scale in military power. He suggests that the overwhelmingly large role of central governments probably did not arise because of economies of scale or other efficiencies in all the services they provide. Rather, it has probably arisen mainly because they have had the military or final power, which has given them the capacity to claim for themselves functions that often could have been performed more efficiently by other jurisdictions.

But why has no world government evolved to take control of over a hundred independent countries, and many tens of thousands of local, state, and special-purpose jurisdictions? Olson sees the reasons for this in the diseconomies of scale that would arise in coordinating and controlling vast spaces and numbers of people, and also in the demand for separate jurisdictions because of cultural differences.

FINAL REMARKS

It is doubtful if there can ever be final generalisations on the optimal degree of decentralisation of expenditures on services or on taxation. Federalism is an evolving process.

The economic models can be developed, but they still need further work. They need to look at the political questions of decentralisation. Naturally – but unfortunately – the analyses will get more complex.

REFERENCES

Bolutoglu, K. (1976) 'Fiscal decentralisation: a survey of normative and positive contributions', *Finanzarchiv* 35:1.

Breton, A. and Scott, A.D. (1980) *The Design of Federations* Montreal: Institute for Research on Public Policy.

Buchanan, J.M. (1988) 'Contractarian political economy and constitutional interpretation', *American Economic Review* 78:2.

Esterbauer, F. and Thöni, E. (1981) 'Begriffe und Gesamtfragestellung', in F. Esterbauer and E. Thöni, *Föderalismus und Regionalismus in Theorie und Praxis* Vienna.

Hamlin, A.P. (1985) 'The political economy of constitutional federalism', *Public Choice* 46:2.

Kirsch, G. (1987), 'Einleitung', in G. Kirsch (ed.), *Föderalismus* Stuttgart-New York.

Oates, W. (1972) *Fiscal Federalism* New York: Harcourt Brace Jovanovich.

Olson, M. (1986) 'Toward a more general theory of governmental structure', *American Economic Review* 76:2.

Quigley, J.M. and Rubinfeld D.L. (1986) 'Budget reform and the theory of fiscal federalism', *American Economic Review* 76:2.

Thöni, E. (1986) *Politokomische Theorie des Föderalismus – Eine Kritische Bestandsaufnahme* Baden-Baden.

Tiebout, C.M. (1956) 'A pure theory of local expenditures', *Journal of Political Economy*, 64:5.

Weingast, B.R., Shepsle, K.A. and Johnsen C.H. (1981) 'The political economy of benefits and costs: a neoclassical approach to distributive politics', *Journal of Political Economy* 89:4.

Wiseman, J. (1987) 'The political economy of federalism: a critical appraisal', *Environment and Planning C: Government and Policy* 5:4.

3 Current issues in the theory of fiscal federalism

David King

INTRODUCTION

The theory of fiscal federalism – or the economics of multi-level government – seeks to help policy-makers answer four key questions. First, what powers should be given to subcentral government rather than central government? Secondly, how large should subcentral authorities – that is regional and local authorities – be? Thirdly, how should subcentral authorities be financed? Fourthly, how far does the central government need to control the activities of subcentral authorities in order to prevent them from frustrating its policies, especially its macroeconomic policies?

This paper focuses on three basically separate issues, two chiefly concerned with the first of these four questions and one chiefly concerned with the third. Following a brief overview of local authority functions in western Europe, it considers the roles – or the possible roles – of local authorities as redistributors and as law-makers. Their law-making seems scarcely touched on in the literature, and yet it seems to be of considerable interest; and it is worth noting that local authorities generally do have some powers in this respect.

Then the paper looks at local finance. Following some general comments, it looks particularly at the so-called 'flypaper effect', which refers to a tendency for local authorities to devote most, if not all, of the proceeds of any increase in grant receipts to increased local spending, whereas they might be expected to devote a substantial proportion of any increase in grants to reducing their own tax revenues. Local authorities in most countries rely heavily on grants, so it seems very important to understand how they react to increases in grants.

LOCAL AUTHORITY FUNCTIONS

The conventional wisdom about functions for local authorities is that they can reasonably be entrusted with the provision of certain public goods, that they should be given little or no powers over income redistribution, and they should have no powers at all over the stabilisation of the economy. Like many conventional wisdoms, this one is not wholly satisfactory.

For instance, local authorities actually provide very few public goods at all. To see this, consider Table 3.1 which indicates the main items provided by subcentral authorities in western Europe. Of course such a table fails to bring out the degree of discretion which these authorities have over the various items, but it is still a useful guide to seeing what activities they undertake. Conceivably parks, roads (or at least minor roads), police, justice and town planning could be regarded as public goods. But there are more items which come under the less satisfactory heading of merit goods, notably the various categories of education, health, welfare services and housing, and arguably theatres, museums and, perhaps, sports and leisure pursuits. Some other activities are municipalised on local monopoly grounds, notably urban transport, ports, airports, district heating, water supply and electricity. Yet others are presumably handled by the public sector on externality grounds, for instance refuse services and fire protection. Perhaps local involvement in slaughterhouses is also explained by the fact that there is an external benefit from slaughtering if it is done humanely.

Interestingly, some local activities, notably agriculture etc., commerce and tourism, and indeed some planning activities, are clearly designed to allow local authorities some scope for stimulating economic activity in their areas. This raises the issue of whether the 'regional development' function of local government can be further strengthened. Some central control over this function is needed, chiefly perhaps to regulate the total level of expenditure involved – for local authorities might otherwise spend vast sums competing for an essentially fixed amount of industrial development – and also perhaps to regulate the amounts to be spent in different areas. But why not entrust most of the permitted amounts to local authorities to spend? In this way, different strategies would be tried and the most cost-effective ones could be copied. Moreover, local authorities might try harder than central government; high levels of unemployment seldom, if ever, occur in capital cities, and central bureaucrats living in them may not always appreciate the full extent of such problems in under-developed regions.

REDISTRIBUTION

This brief review of local activities suggests that they have a much wider range of activities than most writers imply. The large number of merit good activities, for instance, reveals that they must have some considerable interest in redistribution, for the final post-budget incomes of many households are very sensitive to the amounts of in-kind transfers they receive by way of education and health services and subsidised housing.

This subcentral involvement in redistribution was encouraged by President Reagan and the 'New Federalism' in the United States. Yet it runs counter to the conventional wisdom. Indeed, recent theoretical work has added to the arguments against subcentral involvement. The traditional view has been that while there may be a case for subcentral participation, to allow for varying preferences in different areas over the degree of redistribution desired, there are two key objections. First, any area which sought to adopt a more progressive regime than its neighbours would be likely to drive away its rich citizens and lure in poor citizens, and so find the situation untenable. Secondly, helping the poor in any area generates benefits to people elsewhere – who gain by knowing that the needs of the poor are being attended to; but if local authorities provide the service, then they are likely to ignore these external benefits, and so under-provide.

More recently, Brown and Oates (1987) have added a further reason for supposing that subcentral responsiblity is likely to lead to under-provision. This stems from the fact that if subcentral authorities do assume responsibility, then the degrees of redistribution will vary and the poor may migrate to the 'best' areas. Suppose that redistribution occurs from a rich majority to a poor minority. The rich – or rather the median voter who is one of them – will vote for more redistribution until the marginal benefit to them of extra help to the poor is just equal to the marginal cost to them in terms of the lost utility from reduced consumption. The amount of redistribution voted for will be less if migration is likely – as it will be with subcentral provision – because any rise in hand-out levels will incur not only the cost of helping the existing poor, but also the extra cost of helping the new 'immigrant' poor.

Such considerations certainly constitute a powerful case against subcentral redistribution. But they prompt two further rather contradictory thoughts. First, if the externality argument is sound, then does it

Table 3.1 Allocation of functions to subcentral authorities in western Europe

Function	*Austria*	*Belgium*	*Denmark*	*France*	*Germany*	*Ireland*	*Italy*	*Luxemburg*	*Netherlands*	*Norway*	*Portugal*	*Spain*	*Sweden*	*Switzerland*	*Turkey*	*UK*
Refuse collection and disposal	X	X	X	X	X	X	X	X	X	X	X	X	X	X	X	X
Slaughterhouses	X	X	X	X	X	X	X	X	X	X		X	X	X	X	X
Theatres, concert halls	X	X	X	X	X		X	X	X	X	X	X	X	X	X	X
Museums, art galleries, libraries	X	X	X	X	X	X	X	X	X	X	X	X	X	X	X	X
Parks and open spaces	X	X	X	X	X	X	X	X	X	X	X	X	X	X	X	X
Sports & leisure pursuits	X	X	X	X	X	X	X	X	X	X	X	X	X	X	X	X
Roads	X	X	X	X	X	X	X	X	X	X	X	X	X	X	X	X
Urban road transport	X		X	X	X		X	X	X	X	X	X	X	X	X	X
Ports		X			X		X		X	X	X		X	X		
Airports					X		X		X	X			X	X		X
District heating	X	X	X	X	X		X		X				X	X	X	
Water supply	X	X	X	X	X	X	X	X	X	X	X	X	X	X	X	X[3]
Agriculture, forestry, fishing, hunting	X	X		X	X		X		X	X	X	X	X	X	X	X
Electricity		X	X		X		X		X	X	X	X	X	X	X	
Commerce	X	X		X	X		X		X		X	X	X	X	X	
Tourism	X	X		X	X		X		X	X	X	X	X	X	X	X
Financial assistance to local authorities	X	X		X	X		X		X			X		X	X	
Security, police	X	X		X	X		X	X	X			X		X	X	X
Fire protection	X	X	X	X	X	X		X	X	X	X	X	X	X	X	X
Justice					X		X					X				X
Pre-school education	X	X	X	X	X		X	X	X	X		X	X	X		X
Primary and secondary education	X	X	X	X[1]	X		X[2]	X	X	X		X	X	X	X	X
Vocational & technical training	X	X		X	X		X		X	X		X	X	X		X
Higher education		X			X		X					X		X		X
Adult education	X	X	X	X	X		X		X	X		X	X	X		X

Function	*Austria*	*Belgium*	*Denmark*	*France*	*Germany*	*Ireland*	*Italy*	*Luxemburg*	*Netherlands*	*Norway*	*Portugal*	*Spain*	*Sweden*	*Switzerland*	*Turkey*	*UK*
Hospitals and convalescent homes	X	X	X	X	X		X	X	X	X		X	X	X	X	
Personal health	X	X	X	X	X		X	X	X	X		X	X	X	X	
Family welfare services	X	X	X	X	X		X		X	X		X	X	X	X	X
Welfare homes	X	X	X	X	X		X	X	X	X		X	X	X	X	X
Housing	X	X		X	X	X	X	X	X	X	X	X	X	X	X	X
Town planning	X	X	X	X	X	X	X	X	X	X	X	X	X	X	X	X

Source: HMSO, p.131; the author has amended the entry for Portugal and added one for Spain

Notes:
1 Mainly primary education
2 Primary education only
3 Scotland only

apply beyond countries as well as beyond local authorities? If so, is there then an argument that in the EC, say, having poverty relief at a national level rather than an international level leads to too little relief?

Secondly, if adopting an international approach is rejected, then can we help to rescue a subnational approach by means of an effective equalization scheme? If an area which considered doing more to help the poor was deterred by the thought of attracting more poor people, then perhaps the deterrent effect could be reduced or removed by a grant scheme which would acknowledge that the needs of the area had risen, and hence that it deserved more central aid.

It is worth concluding this discussion by noting that much subcentral interference in distribution takes place by means of merit good provision rather than cash transfers. Perhaps the degree to which such in-kind redistribution varies between areas is often constrained by stringent minimum standards requirements. Yet there is still a case to be made for subcentral provision to cater for different types of provision – for instance different education policies, different ways of delivering medical services, and so on.

LAW-MAKING

Earlier sections have suggested that local authorities may do rather more redistributing than the theory recommends. There is arguably a similar gap between practice and theory when it comes to making regulations, because local authorities usually do have some powers in this area, yet the literature seems to ignore it almost entirely.

Or does it? For the theoretical literature often focuses on local public goods, and it is arguable that laws come closer to exhibiting the properties of public goods than almost anything else. To see this, suppose, for instance, that a local authority imposed a 50 kph speed limit on all minor roads in its area. The effects would be non-rival: the fact that they would apply to one particular person does not prevent them applying to all. And the effects would be non-excludable, in the sense that no private producer could offer this facility and prevent people benefiting – perhaps through a fall in road accidents – if they did not pay him! Of course, the law might not be a pure local public good, for it would have some impact on non-residents.

Irrespective of the theoretical niceties, permitting regulations to be made at subcentral level seems to offer the same advantages as permitting some publicly-provided services to be handled at this level. First, it allows for differences between different areas to cater for different tastes. Secondly, people who feel strongly can locate in whichever area suits them best. Thirdly, it facilitates experiments – for different areas are likely to try different ideas.

It is worth considering some areas of life in which a case could be made for extending the powers that subcentral authorities usually have for making regulations. Consider crime, which is a major concern in almost all countries. Should local authorities be able to impose stiffer penalties in their areas? This would surely help to show whether stiffer penalities really were a deterrent. It might be most appropriate to start by allowing local authorities discretion over the length of prison sentences; the central government could perhaps 'charge' local authorities the costs of keeping people in prison for longer than certain 'normal' sentences, so that the authorities would have to match any benefits from greater deterrence against the greater cost of keeping people in custody for longer periods. Of course, if stiffer penalties were imposed in one area in an effort to reduce crime, then there might be the problem that criminals would be diverted elsewhere, creating external effects. Would other areas feel obliged to raise their penalties too? Or would they bribe the first area to go easy.

It is perhaps worth reflecting that one of the few western democracies to retain the death penalty is the United States, where its use is decreed by some states. It is not used in the United Kingdom, despite substantial public support. Is this, perhaps, evidence that subcentral governments do more closely react to voter preferences? In fact, there is a further externality issue here, for some conceivable sentences – say limb amputations for theft, or death for murder – might be sought in one area and upset people elsewhere. It is not clear where property rights lie here. Should the 'barbaric' area bribe others to allow it to carry on, or should other areas bribe it to stop? In practice, of course, such punishments could always be forbidden by the central government.

Of course crime is not deterred by penalties alone. The risk of detection is also relevant (see King and Shone, 1987). Is there, then, a case for allowing local authorities greater discretion over whether to issue random breath tests for motorists? Or for allowing them to offer rewards to people who supply useful information to the police? Should people who drop litter be liable for on-the-spot fines imposed by street cleaners, as – according to a report in *The Times* (16 April 1988) – happens in Dubrovnic?

Next, consider the social services. It has already been shown that local authorities have considerable interest in this area, and that an advantage of decentralisation is that it facilitates variety. But could there be more variety? In education, for instance, should local authorities be allowed to decide whether to give 'free' schooling in publicly-owned schools, or whether to give parents money to pay for education at privately-owned schools? Should they be allowed any influence over the policies adopted by schools, for instance in their attitudes to selection, religion, syllabus or management? And if it is felt inappropriate to tolerate differences between local authorities, then for how long will it be appropriate to tolerate differences between different countries in the EC? Again, what is at issue is externalities; for there is a tendency to suppose that people care about what happens in other local authorities of their own country but not about what happens in other countries. Maybe this is true to some extent – but can it be wholly true?

Another quite separate area for regulations would be on what might broadly be termed environmental issues. In the United Kingdom, at least, local authorities have a little discretion over the hours during which shops can or must be open, and a little discretion over the hours during which alcoholic drinks may be bought for immediate consumption. Should these powers be extended, so that, for instance, Sunday opening could be strictly forbidden in religious areas and alcohol available only in strictly defined periods in areas where local people preferred it that way? Should local authorities be encouraged to levy congestion charges on motorists who use busy streets? To reduce litter, should they be allowed to ban the sale of all drinks unless there was a returnable deposit on the container?

The list of questions could be extended to various other more moral fields. Should local authorities be allowed to decide whether people may indulge in blood sports such as hunting, shooting, fishing or bullfighting? Should they be allowed to decide whether casinos and betting shops may be established?

In considering whether any of these regulatory functions should be given to subcentral government, it is really necessary to ask what is the optimal size of authority to handle them. Clearly some level of government will have control, and the question is whether the optimal size is for an area with a population of several million – which would point to national provision, perhaps even to joint international control – or for an area with a population of, say, less than a million – which would point to subcentral control.

To ascertain the optimal size area for any function, it is helpful to suppose that a given population – say a country or a continent – could in principle be split into areas of any size. One possibility would be 'individual-sized' areas, each with one person. The main advantages of group provision over individual provision are that group decisions will take account of externalities between people within the group and – if service provision is involved – group provision may result in economies of scale. The main disadvantage is loss of individual control. The optimum size occurs when the marginal benefit from any increase just equals the marginal cost.

Now with service provision, economies of scale could play an important part in determining optimum size. Indeed, much of the reason for alliances such as NATO is that even individual countries are too small to exhaust economies of scale in defence. But with most of the law-making functions so far considered, economies of scale are essentially irrelevant: they really occur only with social services if these are provided locally – and even then are probably exhausted fairly quickly.

The absence of an economy of scale effect should encourage investigation to see if local authorities, perhaps quite small ones, are appropriate for many legislative functions. A reasonable supposition is that the optimal size will be close to one which enables external effects between people who live fairly close to be exhausted. People may want stiff penalties for robbers in their street or local town – it matters less to them if robbers a hundred miles away are treated softly. People may want public provision of schools in their own area – in which case the area should perhaps be large enough to warrant a few schools – but it matters less what happens a few towns away. People may (or may not) want local shops open on Sunday, or to be able to place bets – but again what happens in the next town is of limited interest.

This analysis is necessarily tentative. It seeks only to show that here is an area worthy of more investigation than it has so far received. As a first step, it would be interesting to list some of the more important regulatory powers that have been devolved in different countries. But the analysis has an interesting political implication. The growing interdependence of the EC countries is already threatening to lead to central governments losing power to the European parliament. So central governments can certainly be expected to resist losing any other powers to subcentral governments. Yet it may be that in the long run – or perhaps in the very long run – there will be a growing trend for more international decision-taking and for more devolution, so that it is central governments like today's which will become redundant. This should not surprise us. These governments are concerned with areas whose boundaries were drawn up long ago – usually after a war. That does not necessarily mean that those boundaries are rational ones for any government functions.

SUBCENTRAL FINANCE

One advantage of devolving regulatory powers to subcentral authorities is that such powers may not require much subcentral finance. In contrast, local service provision does require substantial local finance, and the almost constant changes in local financial arrangements suggest that governments find it hard to devise satisfactory arrangements.

In this paper it is possible to refer only to revenue on current accounts, which generally comes from user charges, taxes and grants. Only occasionally – for instance in Italy – are local authorities allowed to make much use of loans to finance current spending. There are, however, sound reasons for trying to avoid using loans in this way; for they can lead to overspending as they tend to result in some of the burden of the spending enjoyed by today's citizens being passed on to tomorrow's citizens (King, 1984).

There seems to be growing interest in user charges. The United Kingdom government, for instance, promised in 1986 to conduct a review to see if charges could play a greater role there (HMSO,

1986). No results of this review have been announced, but perhaps the Government will be encouraged by the results of a public opinion survey conducted in the United States in 1987. This survey asked people how they would most like increases in public spending to be financed; respondents had to select one means of finance from a specific list of options. The results for local authorities are given in Table 3.2. They showed that extra charges received more support – 33 per cent of all respondents – than any particular local tax; though rather more people – 38 per cent of all respondents – would have preferred raising one tax or another to extra charges. Interestingly, the same survey showed rather less support – only 13 per cent of respondents – for charges at the state level; but this was doubtless because at that level one option was extra cigarette and liquor taxes, and this option was chosen by 54 per cent of respondents, including, presumably, all non-smokers and light drinkers (ACIR, 1987). Support for charges was also limited at the central government level – 15 per cent; but this was doubtless because at that level one option was a lottery, which was chosen by 47 per cent. Perhaps the implications of local lotteries need further investigation. There could be plenty of revenue-exporting if an area with generous prizes was prepared to take bets from non-residents as well as residents. And maybe local revenues would rise further if all other forms of betting were controlled or banned!

Table 3.2 Answers in a US survey to 'If your local government decided to raise a small amount of addition revenue . . ., which one of these would you prefer?'

	Option	*% support*
1	Raise extra revenue from local income tax	9
2	Raise extra revenue from local sales tax	20
3	Raise extra revenue from local property tax	9
4	Raise extra revenue from user charges[1]	33
5	Object to raising extra revenue[2]	17
6	Don't know	12
	Total	100

Source: ACIR (1987), Table 16

Notes:

1 For instance on local parks, swimming pools, parking, libraries, refuse collection and ambulance services.

2 This option was not actually offered on the questionnaires.

There is a good case for some international comparisons of charging practices, but whatever lessons can be learned there is likely to remain a substantial need for taxes and/or grants. It is, of course, possible to rely almost wholly on grants, as for instance in Belgium and Italy, but there are two clear disadvantages in such an arrangement. First, the fact that central governments pay a large slice of local costs means they are likely to feel justified in laying down rules about how these sums can be spent. Second, the lack of any local taxes makes it very hard for local authorities to spend more – or less – money in response to local wishes.

There is a wide array of local (as opposed to state) taxes in use throughout the world. But a study of these taxes and their yields produces some clear results. First, the 1988 yields of local taxes in relation to GDP exceeded 5 per cent only in the Scandinavian countries – Denmark, Finland, Norway and Sweden – where local authorities rely almost wholly on local income taxes, along with Switzerland, where local authorities rely substantially on a local income tax. Ignoring Austria and Germany, where local taxes are chiefly unalterable shares of central taxes, the only other countries with local tax yields exceeding 3 per cent of GDP were Canada and the United Kingdom, where local authorities relied solely on property taxes, and the United States, where local authorities rely chiefly on property taxes.

The popularity of local income and property taxes is not hard to explain. It is surely that the only alternatives capable of raising high yields are indirect taxes, which are not very suitable at the local level because a substantial part of any one area's tax might be 'exported', and any variations in tax rates between areas could lead to resource-wasting shopping expeditions; indeed, it could be very hard for any one area to have a tax rate much higher than its neighbours' rates.

Nevertheless, there seems to be an upper tolerable limit to property tax rates. Property tax payments were highest in the United Kingdom, where they exceeded 4 per cent of GDP, but here the tax on domestic property has been replaced – albeit apparently for only a few years – by a 'community charge' or poll tax. After the United Kingdom, property tax payments are highest in the United States, at around 2.5 per cent of GDP, yet even there there have been moves – most notably California's Proposition 13 – which have sought to cut the property tax burden.

Why are property taxes so unpopular? Probably one reason is that they are very visible. This feature is now shared by the United

Kingdom's poll tax. However, it is a feature which economists would surely not fault, for it means that voters will be well aware of the costs of local services.

Another objection to property taxes is that they are widely felt to be unfair. There is a tendency for the burden – at least on domestic property – to be regressive; this tendency may be offset to some degree by rebates or circuit-breakers, but the mere existence of these palliatives is a recognition of a problem with the tax. In this context, it is interesting to note the responses to the rather elliptical question 'which do you think is the worst tax – that is the least fair?', given by respondents in a 1987 survey in the United States. Twenty-four per cent of respondents chose the local property tax, while 30 per cent chose the federal income tax (ACIR, 1987). It might be expected that high yielding taxes will fare badly in such surveys, so it is interesting to see that the local property tax was nearly as unpopular as the federal income tax, even though the former has a much smaller yield than the latter.

A poll tax, too, may be felt to be unfair, so it is doubtful if a community charge could ever be expected to raise much more than 2 per cent or so of GDP, about the level which applied in 1990–91 in the United Kingdom. High local tax yields must, it seems, rely on local income taxes, perhaps in combination with other taxes. One advantage of having a poll tax as one of several local taxes would be to ensure that all local voters paid some local taxes directly.

THE FLYPAPER EFFECT

Some standard objections to grant finance have already been noted. More recently, it has been argued that another objection to grants is that they can cause overspending, at least if local authorities also have some tax power of their own. This objection arises out of what is known as the 'flypaper effect', a phenomenon most publicised in the United States. For it appears there that if the federal government raises the incomes of people in an area by cutting its own taxes, then they devote little of their extra spending power to subcentral authority services; yet if the federal government raises their spending power by means of grants to subcentral authorities, then almost all the extra goes on subcentral services! (See Gramlich, 1977 and Stine, 1985). It seems that federal money tends to stick in whichever sector – private or subcentral – it is thrown at, hence the term 'flypaper effect'.

This result may not seem altogether surprising, yet it contradicts what may be termed the standard theory of grants. Here, typically, a median voter is depicted deciding on the allocation of the income in an area – that is the total income available to its citizens, including any income such as grants acquired by its authority from outside the area – between authority spending and private spending. It seems that if the area's income rises, whether as a result, say, of cuts in central taxes causing private disposable incomes to rise or of rises in central grants causing the authority's income to rise, then the median voter should react by opting for the same allocation of the rise between private and authority spending.

A number of explanations for the flypaper effect have been offered (King, 1984, has a survey). These are not exclusive, in that each could be relevant. One particularly interesting model put forward by Oates (1979) sees the median voter suffering from fiscal illusion. Suppose there is one local service, X, and that there are no grants; and suppose the median voter must pay a fixed share of local taxes. Suppose, too, that X is available at a constant unit cost. Then AA' in Figure 3.1 shows the tax price to the median voter of each unit of X. In effect, the median voter regards AA' as the supply curve for X. Initially he selects quantity OQ_1 where AA' cuts his demand curve DD'. If incomes rise generally, and if the median voter's income rises with them, then his demand curve will shift, say to EE', causing him to opt for OQ_2 units. If, instead, the authority receives a lump-sum grant, then it may deceive the voter into thinking that the supply curve is now BB'; BB' certainly shows the new taxprice of X, but it does not show its true cost, which is still shown by AA'. This deception could cause the voter to opt for OQ_3. It is highly likely that OQ_3 will exceed OQ_2; the easiest way of grasping this is to consider how likely it is that the whole income rise or the whole grant rise would be devoted to X. The whole income rise would be devoted to X only if the income elasticity of demand for private goods was zero, which is inconceivable. The whole grant rise would be devoted to X if the price-elasticity of demand for X was one, so that tax revenues at Q_3 (OQ_3GC) equalled tax revenues at Q_1 (OQ_1FA); this is quite feasible. To consider the effect of matching grants, consider an equal value matching grant. With such a grant, the voter would have been tricked into thinking the new supply curve was CC', but he would again have gone to OQ_3; in each case the local budget is OQ_3HA with local taxes of OQ_3GC and grants of $CGHA$.

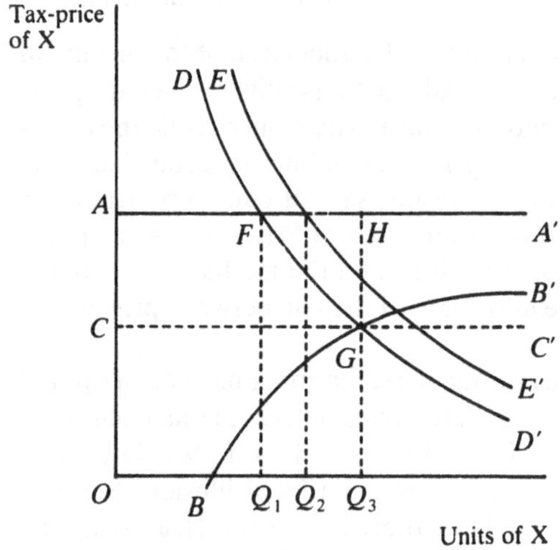

Figure 3.1 The Oates model of the fly-paper effect

A drawback of this model, and most others, is that it implies that lump-sum grants have as much effect as equal-value matching grants, whereas the literature seems to suggest that the latter have more effect (see Gramlich, 1977, and Gramlich and Rubinfeld, 1982). In 1984 I put forward a model of the flypaper effect which is consistent with this result. It, too, can be best explained by supposing there is one local service, X. Suppose that the median voter's preferences between X and private spending are, broadly, reflected by the indifference curves shown in Figure 3.2.

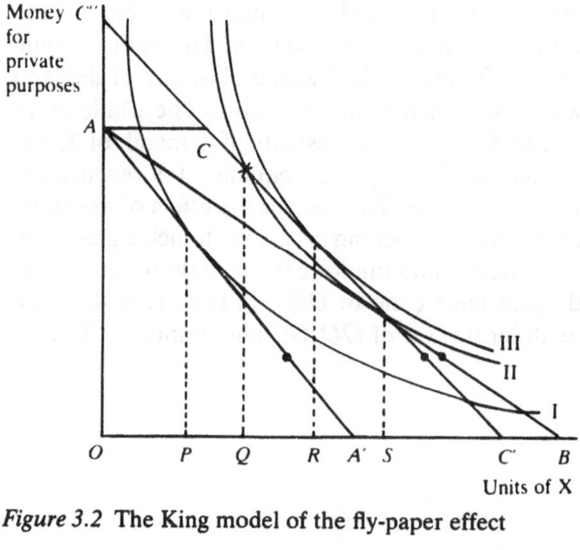

Figure 3.2 The King model of the fly-paper effect

However, the median voter is also concerned by the impact of local taxes on the poor and sets an upper constraint on the level of local taxes. Initially, local income is shown by budget line AA', and this concern with the poor creates an upper tolerable limit on local taxes, and hence on units of X, shown by the spot on AA'. In fact the voter opts for OP units of X – taken from indifference curve I – which is *below* this limit; so the limit is irrelevant.

The receipt of lump-sum grants would create the new budget line ACC'. The upper limit on X is now shown by a spot on CC' at the same horizontal level as before – reflecting the same minimum level of private spending as determined by the same upper constraint on local taxes. The median voter would select OR units of X – taken from indifference curve III; again the limit is irrelevant. With an equal-value matching grant the budget line would be AB. The upper limit on X is shown by a spot on AB which is at the same height as the other spots. This limit is irrelevant in practice, here, as the voter opts for OS units – taken from indifference curve II. Note that the matching grant has more effect. Its equal value is reflected by the fact that ACC' intersects AB above the chosen point, S, on AB; in other words, this point would be available with either grant.

What happens if income rises? Say central taxes are cut, with little benefit to the poor. The budget line will be $C''C'$, but the limit is now depicted by a cross only a little to the right of the spot on AA'. The fact that the poor have gained little means the median voter will tolerate little increase in local taxes, and so little increase in the provision of X. Given $C''C'$, the voter would like OR units of X – taken from indifference curve III – but is constrained to have no more than OQ. For simplicity, OQ is shown as being on indifference curve II. The income rise has less effect – at OQ – than the equal-value grants – at OR or OS.

Interestingly, the recent trend in grants in the United States has been downwards. Has this led to a sharp fall in state and local spending? No – it seems the fall in grants has been largely offset by rises in subcentral taxes. Thus 'by the end of 1986, total state and local spending accounted for the same share of GNP as in 1980, the beginning of the [grant] cutback period' (Gramlich, 1987).

One possible explanation might seem to be that central taxes fell in step with grants. However, the flypaper evidence suggests that the fall in grants would have more effect on local spending than any rise in disposable income. And, in any case, central taxes did *not* fall. Grants were cut to help reduce the federal deficit.

Another possibility is that there is a very high income elasticity of demand for state and local services. If so, then the general rise in GNP could have led to a rise in demand which more than offset the fall in grants. Note, though, that state and local spending would rise in line with GNP if the income elasticity of demand were unity and if grants *rose* in line with GNP. The income elasticity would have to be well in excess of unity for spending to rise in line with GNP – as observed – if grants actually fell.

It is interesting to note that the model of grant effects explained in relation to Figure 3.2 offers another possible explanation of why state and local taxes might have risen. To see this, consider Figure 3.3. Suppose that in 1980 an authority had the budget line *ACC′* – taken to include some grants – and that the median voter's limit was at the point marked by a spot. Then he would be constrained by the limit to choose *OP* units of X – on indifference curve III; the limit is binding here. Notice, incidentally, that a modest rise in grants would be devoted entirely to X while a modest cut in central taxes might be devoted chiefly to private spending.

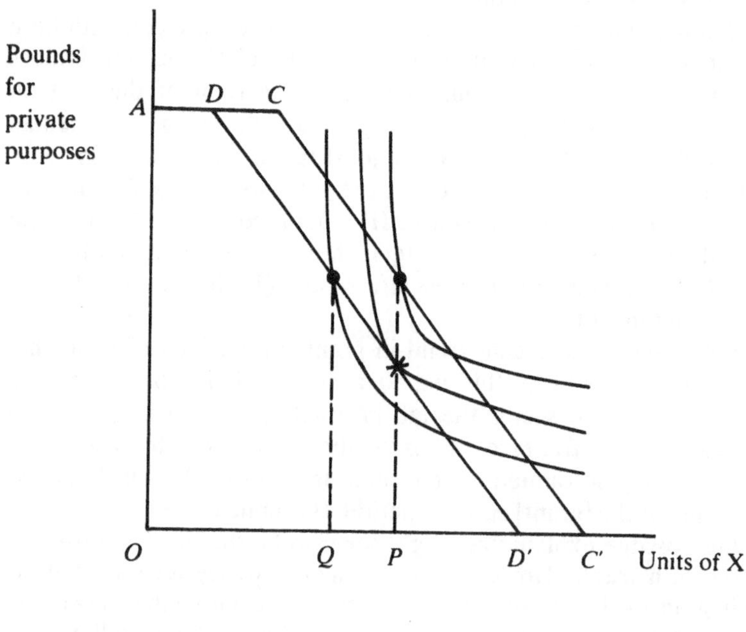

Figure 3.3 The possible effect on United States local authority budgets of the 1980s cuts in grants

Now a cut in grants between 1980 and 1986 would shift the budget line to *ADD′* and the constraint to the point on *DD′* marked with a spot. This is to the left of the old constraint, to reflect the same minimum level of private spending, that is the same upper limit on subcentral taxes. It would be expected that the median voter would opt for *OQ* units of X – on indifference curve I – which represents a sharp fall from *OP*.

But suppose that over the same period the median voter became less concerned by the impact of subcentral taxes on the poor. Then, by 1986, the constraint could move downwards, showing a willingness to impose higher non-central taxes. Conceivably, by 1986, it would be at the position on *DD′* marked with a cross. If so, then the median voter would once more opt for *OP* units of X, though he would now be on indifference curve II. More broadly, allowing that incomes rose in the 1980–6 period, the median voter might well have opted for subcentral spending to account for the same proportion of GNP that applied in 1980 without having to have an especially high income elasticity of demand for such spending.

The crucial question, then, is whether concern over the impact of subcentral taxes on the poor has fallen. Arguably, this is not far from asking whether concern with property taxes has fallen, for property taxes – or at least domestic property taxes – are typically felt to be an exceptionally unfair subcentral tax; that is why there are circuit breakers in the United States and why there were rate rebates in the United Kingdom.

Some evidence that concern with property taxes may have fallen in the United States is offered by Table 3.3. This shows the results of surveys conducted over the years 1972–87 to see what people consider to be the least fair tax: for simplicity, the table shows averages for three-year periods. A limitation of this approach is that the numbers might stay the same over time even if all taxes were felt to be becoming more or less fair. Even so, it is striking that the local property tax is no longer felt to be the worst tax. It used to be felt to be by far the worst, but is now way behind the federal income tax.

No doubt a key reason for the apparent fall in concern with property taxes is their falling importance. As a percentage of revenues for all United States' city governments, the local property tax fell from 27.9

Table 3.3 Percentages of respondents in a US survey indicating particular taxes as the 'worst' – that is 'the least fair'[1]

Period	*1972–4* %	*1975–8*[2] %	*1979–81* %	*1982–4* %	*1985–7* %
Federal income tax	26	29	36	36	35
State income tax	11	11	9	11	10
State sales tax	18	19	16	14	18
Local property tax	35	31	28	28	25
Don't know	12	10	11	11	12

Source: ACIR (1987), pp.16–21

Notes:

1 Totals may not add to 100 owing to rounding errors.

2 Covers three years only, as no survey in 1976.

per cent in 1970 to 16.7 per cent in 1983 (King, 1988); instead, cities have relied more on items such as charges and sales taxes. And at state level, where property taxes are admittedly less important, they waned between 1960 and 1982, falling from 3.4 per cent of tax revenue to 1.9 per cent (Feenberg and Rosen, 1986); instead, states relied much more on income taxes and sales taxes. Quite apart from falling in importance, property taxes may also have been felt to have become less unfair as a result of the continued development of circuit-breakers. Interestingly, rebates in the United Kingdom have – until 1988 – covered 100 per cent of the rate payments of the poorest people. This may well have eased the concern of median voters in the UK and help explain their willingness over the period 1976–86 to allow the local property tax to rise enough to maintain 1986 current spending at about 12.7 per cent of GDP, despite a significant fall in central government grants.

It is appropriate to end this analysis with two further thoughts. First, there may, of course, be other factors helping to explain the apparent non-reversibility of the flypaper effect in the United States. For instance, it is notoriously harder to cut public spending than it is to raise it. And cutting public spending rapidly typically leads to redundancies for some public employees. Perhaps median voters care about this just as they may care about the poor.

Table 3.4 Net domestic rates and net community charge payments in England as percentages of net household income (1986–7 prices)

Range of net household income (£ per week)	*Net rates (%)*	*Net charge (%)*
Under 50	4.1	3.4
50–75	4.4	3.7
75–100	4.6	4.4
100–150	4.7	4.6
150–200	4.0	4.0
200–250	3.4	3.4
250–300	3.0	3.0
300–350	2.7	2.7
350–400	2.6	2.5
400–500	2.3	2.2
Over 500	2.1	1.7
All households	3.3	3.2

Source: Department of the Environment, *News Release 16* (13 January 1988)

Secondly, it may be wondered if concern with the poor will grow in the United Kingdom, now that the domestic property tax has been replaced by a poll tax on adults. Given the frequent allegations in the press that the poll is unfair, such a growth in concern would seem inevitable. However, the poll tax is kind to single-adult households, and most of the poorest households have only one adult. Table 3.4 – which allows for rebates with both taxes – indicates that low income households will in fact be better off with the poll tax than they were with rates. On this basis, there is no reason to expect a major growth in concern about the effect of local taxes on the very poor. In turn, there is no reason to expect such concern to lead to a substantial flypaper effect. Consequently, the government may continue to find that its downward pressure on grants has limited downward effect on local authority spending.

REFERENCES

ACIR (1987) *Changing Public Attitudes on Governments and Taxes* Washington: Advisory Commission on Intergovernmental Relations.

Brown, C.C. and Oates, W.E. (1987) 'Assistance to the poor in a federal system', *Journal of Public Economics* 32:3.

Feenberg, D.R. and Rosen, H.S. (1986) 'State personal income and sales taxes, 1977–1983', in H.S. Rosen (ed.) *Studies in State and Local Public*

Finance, Chicago: Chicago University Press.
Gramlich, E.M. (1977) 'Intergovernmental grants: a review of the empirical literature', in W.E. Oates (ed.) *The Political Economy of Fiscal Federalism* Lexington, Mass.: Lexington Books.
——(1987) 'Federalism and federal deficit reduction', *National Tax Journal* 40:3.
Gramlich, E.M. and Rubinfeld, D.L. (1982) 'Micro estimates of public spending demand functions and tests of the Tiebout and median-voter hypotheses', *Journal of Political Economy* 90:3.
HMSO (1986) *Paying for Local Government*, Green Paper, Cmnd.9714, London: HMSO.
King, David (1984) *Fiscal Tiers: the Economics of Multi-Level Government*, London: Allen & Unwin.
King, David and Shone, R. (1987) *Microeconomics: an Introduction to Theory and Applications*, London: Edward Arnold.
King, Desmond (1988) 'Sources of local finance in the United States', in R. Paddison and S. Bailey (eds) *Local Government Finance: International Perspectives*, London: Routledge.
Oates, W.E. (1979) *Intergovernmental Grants and Revenue Sharing: Theory and Evidence*, Public Sector Economic Research Centre Discussion Paper 79–07, Leicester: University of Leicester.
Stine, W.F. (1985) 'Estimating the responsiveness of local revenue to intergovernmental aid', *National Tax Journal* 38:2.

4 Local finance in Spain

Present structure and prospects for applied research

Antoni Castells and Joaquim Sole-Vilanova

INTRODUCTION

This paper is divided into two parts. The first part describes the system of finance of local government in Spain and its future development. The second part selects some significant topics from the theory of fiscal federalism and its applications, and suggests the results which would be expected in an applied analysis of Spanish local authorities.

Applied studies on Spanish local finance are relatively few. There are several reasons for this: first the neglect and the relative unimportance of the local public sector between 1925 and 1978; secondly, the radical political and constitutional changes which took place in Spain in the period 1975–88; thirdly, the lack of disaggregated data; and, finally, the fact that the potential researchers of the last twenty years have been policy-orientated.

THE STRUCTURE AND FINANCE OF LOCAL GOVERNMENT

The new Spanish Constitution of 1978 retained the two-tier local government system – provinces and municipalities – that was established at the beginning of the nineteenth century. However, local authorities have now a double dependence: on the central government and on the seventeen newly-created regional governments or 'autonomous communities'. Local authorities are now regulated both by the Local Government Act approved by the central parliament in 1985 and by any legislation that regional parliaments may pass.

Since the constitutional reform and the later creation of seventeen regional governments, the provincial level has been in a process of adaptation to the new situation. Formally, the number of provinces has been reduced from fifty to forty-three, seven of the previous provinces having become autonomous communities. However, the

Table 4.1 Size of municipalities in Spain, 1986

Autonomous Community	*Population:* *Less than 2,000*		*2,000–5,000*		*5,000–20,000*		*20,000–100,000*		*100,000–500,000*		*More than 500,000*		*All municipalities*	
	no.	*%*	*no.*	*%*	*no.*	*%*	*no.*	*%*	*no.*	*%*	*no.*	*%*	*no.*	*%*
ANDALUSIA	306	40.0	225	29.4	177	23.2	47	6.2	7	0.9	2	0.3	764	100
ARAGON	673	92.6	34	4.7	17	2.3	2	0.3	–	–	1	0.1	727	100
ASTURIAS	23	29.5	21	26.9	24	30.8	8	10.2	2	2.6	–	–	78	100
BALEARIC I.	17	25.8	23	34.8	21	31.8	4	6.1	1	1.5	–	–	66	100
CANARY I.	8	9.2	24	27.6	41	47.1	11	12.6	3	3.5	–	–	87	100
CANTABRIA	56	54.9	30	29.4	14	13.7	1	1.0	1	1.0	–	–	102	100
CASTILE-LEON	2,111	93.9	90	4.0	35	1.5	8	0.4	4	0.2	–	–	2,248	100
CASTILE-LA MANCHA	749	81.8	104	11.4	50	5.4	12	1.3	1	0.1	–	–	916	100

CATALONIA	677	72.0	128	13.6	94	10.0	32	3.4	8	0.9	1	0.1	940	100
ESTREMADURA	258	67.9	79	20.8	36	9.5	6	1.6	1	0.2	–	–	380	100
CALICIA	26	8.3	129	41.3	140	44.9	14	4.5	3	1.0	–	–	312	100
MADRID	119	66.8	21	11.9	17	9.5	14	7.9	6	3.4	1	0.5	178	100
MURCIA	6	13.3	4	8.9	25	55.6	8	17.8	2	4.4	–	–	45	100
RIOJA	156	89.7	11	6.3	6	3.4	–	–	1	0.6	–	–	174	100
VALENCIA	329	61.4	79	14.7	88	16.4	36	6.7	3	0.6	1	0.2	536	100
NAVARRE	213	80.4	40	15.1	10	3.8	1	0.4	1	0.4	–	–	265	100
BASQUE COUNTRY	142	60.2	29	12.3	47	19.9	14	5.9	4	1.7	–	–	236	100
Ceuta & Melilla	–	–	–	–	–	–	2	100.0	–	–	–	–	2	100
SPAIN: municipalities (number)	5,869	72.9	1,071	13.3	842	10.4	220	2.7	48	0.6	6	0.1	8,056	100
SPAIN: population (thousands)	3,166	8.2	3,287	8.5	7,731	20.1	8,139	21.2	8,873	23.1	7,277	18.9	38,473	100

Source: Instituto Nacional de Estadistica, Madrid

Local Government Act of 1985 defines the minimum responsibilities of provincial authorities: first, to offer technical and economic assistance to municipalities, and second to provide what may be considered supramunicipal services.

As is shown in Table 4.1, Spain has 8,056 municipalities (*municipios*). Over 86.2 per cent of these municipalities have fewer than 5,000 inhabitants together accounting for only 16.7 per cent of the total population. In contrast, 63.2 per cent of the population are located in municipalities of more than 20,000 inhabitants.

About one thousand municipalities whose populations had declined were amalgamated or absorbed by larger ones in the period 1960–75. However, as in many southern European countries, implementing a comprehensive policy of municipality amalgamation would have had a high political cost which would be almost prohibitive. This is because the mobility of individuals is very low and people have a strong consciousness of local identity. Some alternatives to amalgamation were the creation of the metropolitan council of Barcelona in 1974, which has recently been reformed by the regional government of Catalonia, and the setting-up of a new supramunicipal level of government (*comarcas*), also in Catalonia, in 1988.

The variety of the size of the municipalities makes an efficient allocation of responsibilities very unlikely. Small municipalities have great difficulties with the production and provision of many services and also with tax collection and financial management. The Local Government Act of 1985 established the criterion that the level of compulsory responsibilities of municipal authorities sshould increase according to the population. This flexibility in the allocation of responsibilities is quite reasonable, although it is not clear that the higher levels of government allocate to small municipalities all the services they need in order to avoid any territorial discrimination between individuals living in different jurisdictions.

Turning now to finance, it is convenient to take provincial governments and municipalities in turn. The tax power of provincial governments is almost non-existent. Provinces are allowed to levy only a limited surcharge on the municipal business tax. The main sources of provincial finance are two unconditional grants from the central government. The major grant is now formally a substitute for the previous tax-share of the central government's general sales tax; this was abolished in 1986 when the new value added tax was introduced. From 1989 both unconditional grants have been unified and distributed according to population and other need variables.

(Provinces also receive a capital grant which is distributed between the municipalities as project grants.) Table 4.2 shows the financial dependence of provinces on grants, which represented 84 per cent of total receipts in 1986.

Table 4.2 The structure of municipal and provincial finance, 1986

	Municipalities		*Provinces*[1]
Revenue item	20,000– *50,000 pop.*	100,000– *500,000 pop.*	
	%	%	%
Own revenue	61.28	61.08	15.75
Taxes:	29.67	33.91	6.22
Property taxes	17.87	19.27	–
Business taxes	6.48	9.22	6.22
Vehicle tax	4.70	5.14	–
Excise taxes	0.62	0.28	–
Fees, charges and fines	28.90	24.52	5.45
Other own revenues	2.71	2.65	4.08
Grants	38.72	38.91	84.25
Current grants:	29.80	34.63	84.14
Unconditional grants	29.80	34.63	78.95
Specific grants	–	–	5.20
Capital grants	8.92	4.28	0.11
Total revenue	100.00	100.00	100.00

Source: Banco de Credito Local de Espana, Madrid

Note:

1 Sample of the four provinces in the region of Catalonia.

As for municipalities, their traditionally limited taxing power has not been much affected by the constitutional reform. Municipalities have no autonomous power to introduce new taxes, which have to be approved by central or regional parliament. According to a recent decision of the Constitutional Court, this limit applies not only to the description of the tax base, but also to the tax rate or, at least, the upper and the lower limits of the rate that municipalities may levy.

The most important municipal tax is the tax on urban property. Its tax base is defined by the central government, which is also concerned with the assessment of property values. From January 1988, municipal governments have been free to set the tax rate they wish to levy, although this is subject to a lower limit, which is the same for all municipalities, and to an upper limit, which varies according to population. The larger the population of a municipality, the higher the upper limit of its tax rate. Currently, the upper limit for large towns is 4.6 times the lower limit.

Other taxes on property have included the tax on rural property, the vacant site tax, and the capital gains tax on urban property value which is levied when properties are sold. Table 4.2 shows that in 1986 taxes on property represented nearly 20 per cent of municipalities' total revenue, and almost 50 per cent of their revenue from taxes.

The main local business tax is levied on all kinds of business undertakings. The set of tariffs for the different categories of business are regularly fixed and updated by the central government. Municipal governments levy this tax at a rate which may vary between narrow limits. Another tax on businesses has been the business location tax, which until 1989 was levied in all provincial capitals and in all towns with more than 100,000 inhabitants: it was optional in other municipalities. The base for this tax depended on the area occupied by the businesses and their location in the municipality.

The vehicle tax is an important municipal tax. Again, the central government fixes the minimum and the maximum charge for each type of vehicle; each municipality chooses the appropriate tariffs to be levied in its area.

Other municipal taxes have included a luxury consumption tax and an outdoors publicity tax. These two taxes, plus the business location tax and the vacant site tax, were abolished in 1989.

In Spain, fees and charges are quite important at the municipal level. They account for 25 per cent of total revenue in towns with more than 100,000 inhabitants, and may reach 30 per cent in municipalities which have fewer than 20,000 inhabitants. However, the main fees or charges are really concealed taxes. This is the case with charges for refuse collection, building permission and sewerage. In the 1960s and 1970s a very important means of financing urban development used to be special assessments (or betterment levies).

For many years, the municipalities' power to tax has been so limited and their resources so scarce that they have had to make use of fees and charges, even at times to the point of abuse. With the new limited power to fix tax rates and the growing unconditional grants which municipalities have received since the beginning of the 1980s, fees and charges seem to be receding at a time when local user charges are being reconsidered in many other countries.

In recent years an unconditional grant provided by the central government has been the most important source of revenue for the municipalities. The grant comes from the so-called National Fund of Municipal Cooperation, which is financed with a block grant calculated on an annual basis. Municipalities also receive project grants from provincial governments. However, the total amount of grants received by municipal governments does not exceed 40 per cent of their total revenue.

The block grant to Spanish municipalities is distributed to different areas in accordance with their (adjusted) populations, total tax collection and public school units. These three criteria respectively have weights of 70 per cent, 25 per cent and 5 per cent so that the actual formula of distribution is as follows:

$$G_i = BG \left(0.70 \frac{a_i P_i}{\Sigma a_i P_i} + 0.25 \frac{T_i}{\Sigma T_i} + 0.5 \frac{L_i}{\Sigma L_i}\right)$$

where:

- G_i = the grant received by municipality i.
- BG = the total annual block grant allocated by the central government to the National Fund.
- P_i = the population of municipality i.
- a_i = an adjustment coefficient depending on the size of the population ($1 < a < 2.85$) of municipality i.
- T_i = the local tax revenue in municipality i.
- L_i = the number of publicly-funded school units in municipality i.

The adjusted population and school units are proxies for needs. However, the parameter T_i, tax collection, implies that part of the grant is allocated to the municipalities depending on their tax effort and their tax capacity. This implies that the grant does not pursue horizontal equalisation.

Finally, it should be said that during the period of political transition in Spain (1975–83) important deficits were accumulated in some of the large municipalities. The central government helped to redeem these deficits in 1977, 1979, 1980 and 1983. However, it is expected that the unconditional grant to municipalities will increase significantly and that deficits will not occur in future.

APPLIED RESEARCH ON LOCAL GOVERNMENT FINANCE: SETTING THE SCENE

The economic analysis of local government finance covers the three traditional branches of public expenditure – the allocation, the distribution, and stabilisation functions. However, because of the special characteristics of local government, the problems connected with the allocation aspects have probably had a higher profile.

This means that when studies have been made of local finance, there has been a tendency to pay special attention to the problems of allocation. Thus the functions of local governments have been analysed in an attempt to study the gains in efficiency which derive from decentralisation, the optimal size of jurisdiction, and the existence of interjurisdictional externalities or spillovers. Likewise local taxes – especially property taxes – have been examined to see their effect on the location of the factors of production, and grants have been examined to see what influence they have on the level of local expenditure. And equalisation grants have been examined to see what effects they have on redistribution as well as allocation. As has been frequently shown (see, for example, Boadway and Flatters, 1982) in a system with different levels of government, equalisation grants are necessary to equalise the 'fiscal residuum' between persons with the same level of income who reside in different jurisdictions and, therefore, to guarantee allocative efficiency. This reason is additional to the traditional reasons of vertical equity between levels of government and horizontal equity between units of government at the same level. Lotz (1983) is, however, right when he points out that all too often insufficient emphasis has been given to the allocative aspect of equalisation grants.

It is natural that much of the empirical work on local government finance should have centred on allocation problems, although some attention has been paid to redistribution and stabilisation. The aim of the rest of this paper is to summarise the main lines of empirical research on local government finance and to indicate some working hypotheses for future analysis in Spain.

INCIDENCE OF TAXES ON THE PRICE OF FACTORS

One of the most common applications of the Tiebout hypothesis in the empirical field has been the verification of possible capitalisation effects on property values of differences in property tax rates (see, for instance, Oates, 1969, and Hamilton, 1976). Other things being equal, capital invested in immovable property will seek the same net return in different jurisdictions, so the price of property should be lower in the places where the tax is higher.

This type of analysis has concentrated above all on property taxes. This is partly because of the important role played by these taxes at the local level – especially in English-speaking countries – and partly because the high spatial rigidity of the taxed factor makes analysis in this case particularly relevant. However, capitalisation effects may well arise when other taxes are levied. In Spain, empirical research on this question made little sense until recently, because the local authorities had no freedom to make decisions on the property tax rate.

One possible line of research would be to examine the effective tax rate on property, that is the ratio of the actual tax bill to the real value of the property. There are obvious differences in the effective rate throughout a country if, as happens in Spain, there is no homogeneity in the relation between the assessed value for tax purposes and the real value of the property. These differences have tended to increase in recent years with the growth of local discretion in fixing the tax rate. So we can suggest as a working hypothesis that other things being equal (income level, economic activity, town planning regulations, etc.) the value of property will be lower in those areas where the effective rate is higher.

FISCALLY-INDUCED MOBILITY

According to the most generally accepted interpretation of the Tiebout hypothesis, geographical movements of the population are influenced by fiscal factors. Cebula (1979), especially, has produced a useful survey of empirical contributions in this area; and Lotz (1983) has referred to the 'snowball effects' which result from the tendency of different jurisdictions each to attract people with a particular income level.

There is a relatively well-known distortion of the Tiebout model which occurs frequently in real life: the grouping of citizens on the basis of their preferences concerning the public service and tax package (or fiscal basket) is not neutral in respect of income level. If people's groupings in different jurisdictions tend to consolidate different income levels, then this will have an undeniable effect on tax bases and tax rates. In turn it will inevitably affect geographical mobility.

It seems worth investigating whether fiscal differences in Spain have a significant effect on the mobility of citizens. Such differences may perhaps begin to exert a certain influence in the future, although in the past the main factors affecting the location of citizens have been the availability of work, the levels of wages and salaries and the conditions of the housing market.

INTERJURISDICTIONAL FISCAL COMPETITION

Traditional economic analysis has maintained that interjurisdictional fiscal competition – through which each government unit uses its fiscal instruments to attract industry – is disadvantageous for the country, because it is likely to result in a non-optimal location of industry. This has been an argument in favour of fiscal co-ordination and harmonisation, and also of a centralisation of tax powers (Groenewegen, 1988).

The most recent literature seems to emphasise two types of conclusion (McGuire 1986, Shannon 1986 and White 1986). First, differences in local fiscal policies – for instance in grants to businesses and in tax exemptions – have a greater impact than was previously thought on decisions affecting location of investment. Secondly, the negative consequences of tax competition in terms of efficiency are probably less severe than was thought to be the case.

In recent years, a certain importance has been given in Spain to the economic development policies promoted by the municipal governments. Although the possibilities of acting via tax incentives are relatively limited, there are other mechanisms which have been used frequently. The empirical line of research which needs to be developed here is an evaluation of the real effectiveness of these policies for achieving economic growth, considering them in national aggregate terms.

GOVERNMENT STRUCTURES AND OPTIMAL JURISDICTIONS

The problem of the allocation of responsibilities to the different tiers of government assumes an additional dimension when the possibility of congestion costs in the consumption of public goods is introduced into the analysis. Such costs mean these goods may provide benefits which are reduced when the number of consumers rises.

This analysis has led to the development of the theory of clubs, according to which it can be shown that there is for each government function of service an optimal population size (see, for instance, Buchanan, 1965, Litvack and Oates, 1970, Sandler and Tschirhart, 1980, Musgrave and Musgrave, 1980, and Topham, 1981). The difficulties in drawing up useful prescriptions are obvious, and even if it were in fact possible to draw them up, their practical implementation might well lie in the distant future. However, Bahl (1984) is too radical in this context when he claims that neither economic nor political theory provides guidelines for judging the optimal size of government.

There are two certain working hypotheses which ought to be tested: that the social demands made on the local public sector are increasingly diversified, and that the expenditure functions of the local public sector have technical characteristics such that they demand, for their efficient provision, different sizes of jurisdiction.

DECENTRALISATION AND THE SIZE OF THE PUBLIC SECTOR

According to the theorem of decentralisation, decentralisation of the public sector allows benefits to be gained in terms of efficiency by making possible provisions differentiated on the basis of varying preferences. Furthermore, it has been suggested that the intergovernmental competition which goes hand-in-hand with decentralisation encourages a higher level of efficiency than would be found in a situation of strong centralisation.

Studies carried out to test these hypotheses do not present conclusive results. For instance, Cameron (1978) and Nelson (1987) confirm a significant positive relation between the size of the public sector and the degree of decentralisation. However, Oates (1985) considers that the degree of centralisation has no significant bearing on the size of the public sector. This line of research is undoubtedly relevant to the Spanish situation, where there has been an intense decentralisation process in recent years. Hitherto this decentralisation process has been accompanied by a marked growth of the public sector, so that a negative result would be given if a simple test were made of the last hypothesis referred to above. But one has to bear in mind that the factors which have affected the growth of the public sector would have appeared anyway and that, therefore, what is important to analyse is whether this growth would, in the medium term, have been more or less strong if it had not been accompanied by political decentralisation.

EQUALISING CAPACITY OF THE GRANT SYSTEM

According to the most usual interpretations, equalisation grants attempt to guarantee that the tax base differences between jurisdictions do not affect the possibility of different government units providing similar levels of services, on the basis of the needs which they have to meet. The problems connected with the measurement of the indicators of fiscal capacity and fiscal needs are well known (see, for example, Wildasin, 1987) and any empirical research project will of course have to take account of them.

In the Spanish case, the system of unconditional grants which the municipalities receive is not really conceived as a system for horizontal equalisation. The Central Fund is distributed according to need variables and tax effort, but not according to the deficits in tax capacity of the different municipalities. Research will first of all have to attempt to formulate appropriate indicators for fiscal capacity and needs, and, secondly, it will have to examine different possible alternative grant schemes.

REFERENCES

Aaron, J. and Pechman, J.A. (eds) (1981) *How Taxes Affect Economic Behaviour*, Washington: The Brookings Institution.

Aronson, J.R. and Hilley, J.L. (1986) *Financing State and Local Governments*, Washington: The Brookings Institution.

Bahl, R. (1984) *Financing State and Local Government in the 1980s* New York: Oxford University Press.

Boadway, R. and Flatters, F. (1982) *Equalization in a Federal State*, Ottawa: Economic Council of Canada.

Buchanan, J.M. (1965) 'An economic theory of clubs', *Economica* 32:65.

Cameron, D.R. (1978) 'The expansion of the public economy: a comparative analysis', *American Political Science Review* 72:4.

Cebula, R.J. (1979) 'A survey of the literature on the migration impact of state and local government policies', *Public Finance* 34:1.

Cnossen, S.(ed.) (1983) *Comparative Tax Studies*, Amsterdam: North Holland.

Groenewegen, P.D. (1988) 'Taxation and decentralisation: a reconsideration of the costs and benefits of a decentralised tax system' (mimeo).

Hamilton, B.W. (1976) 'The effects of property taxes and local public spending on property values: a theoretical comment', *Journal of Political Economy* 84:3.

Litvack, J.M. and Oates, W.E. (1970) 'Group size and the output of public goods: theory and application to state-local finance in the United States', *Public Finance* 25:1.

Lotz, J.R. (1983) 'The role of local government taxation: the Tiebout effect and equalization' in S. Cnossen (ed.).

McGuire, T.J. (1986) 'Interstate tax differentials, tax competition and tax policy', *National Tax Journal* 39:3.

Musgrave, R.A. and Musgrave, P.B. (1980) *Public Finance in Theory and Practice*, London: McGraw Hill-Kogakusha.

Nelson, M.A. (1987) 'Searching for Leviathan: comment and extension', *American Economic Review* 77:1.

Oates, W.E. (1969) 'The effects of property taxes and local public spending

on property values: an empirical study of tax capitalization and the Tiebout hypothesis', *Journal of Political Economy* 77:5.
——(1985) 'Searching for Leviathan: an empirical study', *American Economic Review* 75:4.
——(1988) 'Decentralization of the public sector: an overview' (mimeo).
Prest, A.R. (1981) *The taxation of urban land*, Manchester: Manchester University Press.
Rosen, H.S. (ed.) (1986) *Studies in State and Local Public Finance*, Chicago: National Bureau of Economic Research, The University of Chicago Press.
Sandler, T. and Tschirhart, J.T. (1980) 'The economic theory of clubs: an evaluative survey', *Journal of Economic Literature* 18:4.
Shannon, J. (1986) 'Interstate tax competition: the need for a new look', *National Tax Journal* 39:3 (September).
Topham, N. (1981) 'Local government economics', in *Public Sector Economics*, London: Longman.
White, M.J. (1986) 'Property taxes and firm location: evidence from proposition 13', in Rosen (1986) pp.83–112.
Wildasin, D.E. (1987) 'Federal-State fiscal relations: a review of the Treasury Report', *Public Finance Quarterly* 15:4.

5 Financing local government

An international perspective with particular reference to local taxation

Jeffrey Owens

INTRODUCTION

The relationship between central, regional and local governments is changing. Some governments are committed to decentralising expenditures and revenues, while others are adopting a more interventionist approach in the affairs of local government. In almost all member countries of the OECD, however, the control and financing of lower levels of government is a major political issue. Many countries have recently implemented (e.g. France and the UK) or are in the process of implementing (e.g. Belgium, Portugal and Spain) major reforms to the ways in which local government is financed. In most cases, these reforms include a reallocation of expenditure functions between levels of government, and in some they include changes in the boundaries of local government units.

The purpose of this paper is to provide an international (OECD) perspective to the current debate on the reform of local taxation. Its main focus is on the use of taxes to finance local government and on the links between central and local government tax systems. The paper does not discuss the appropriate expenditure functions of local government or the related question of the ideal size of local government units. It is clear, however, that these issues need to be resolved prior to deciding upon the ways in which local government should be financed, since the solutions adopted will influence the local revenue structure.

The paper discusses briefly the changing fiscal environment in OECD countries, summarising major tax reforms and the tendency towards a more decentralised approach to government. It then looks at the trends in overall tax levels and structures and in the ways in which state and local governments are financed, before examining the interaction between central and local tax systems. Finally it looks at the current trends in the use of property taxes in OECD countries.

THE CHANGING FISCAL ENVIRONMENT

Taxation now accounts for more than 40 per cent of the gross domestic product in ten OECD countries, and in most countries the burden of taxation has increased significantly (see Table 5.1). Much of the increase has been due to the need to finance the growth in the welfare state. During the 1960s and for most of the 1970s governments extended the scope and generosity of social benefits, and the prevalent attitude was one of optimism as regards the ability of government to resolve social and economic problems. Governments of all political colours adopted an interventionist approach. During recent years the efficacy of government intervention has been increasingly questioned; more emphasis has been placed on the role of market forces and a more neutral stance by government; a consensus has emerged in many countries that the 'size' of government should be cut back, or at least not increased.

Tax policies have not been immune to these changing attitudes. Some governments are examining ways of reducing the level of taxation or, at least, of changing the balance between direct and indirect taxation. Governments and others have grown sceptical about the use of tax expenditures – that is subsidies provided through the tax system – in promoting social and economic goals. Tax structures are being critically reviewed to identify provisions which may be adversely affecting economic decisions. One consequence of these changing attitudes is an increase in proposals to reform tax systems.

Table 5.2 shows that tax reform is on the political agenda in most countries. In the Pacific countries (Australia, New Zealand, Japan and Canada), the debate has focused on the introduction of a broad-base consumption tax (usually some form of VAT). In Canada and Japan, a new tax on consumption is seen as a way to reduce budget deficits, whereas in Australia and New Zealand these taxes are advocated as the key to lowering rates of income tax. To date, only New Zealand has implemented such a tax (the goods and service tax), though there is a fair chance that Canada will introduce a business transfer tax – a form of VAT. Canada is also examining the reduction of corporation tax rates, and Australia and New Zealand are committed to reducing the tax discrimination against distributed profits by partially integrating the personal and corporate income tax system. Each country

Table 5.1 Receipts from main taxes as percentages of GDP at market prices OECD countries, 1975, 1985 and 1986[1]

Country	*Total taxes*			*Personal income tax*			*Corporation income tax*			*Employees' social security*			*Employers' social security*			*General consumption*			*Excises, etc*		
	1975	*1985*	*1986*	*1975*	*1985*	*1986*	*1975*	*1985*	*1986*	*1975*	*1985*	*1986*	*1975*	*1985*	*1986*	*1975*	*1985*	*1986*	*1975*	*1985*	*1986*
Sweden [2]	44	51	54	20	20	20	2	2	3	–	–	–	8	12	13	5	7	7	5	6	5
Denmark [2,3]	41	49	51	23	24	24	1	2	3	–	1	1	–	1	1	7	10	10	6	6	7
Norway [2,3]	45	47	50	14	11	11	1	8	7	2	3	3	8	7	7	9	9	10	7	9	9
Netherlands [2]	44	45	46	12	9	9	3	3	3	7	9	8	8	8	8	6	7	8	4	3	3
Belgium [2]	41	47	45	13	16	15	3	3	3	4	6	6	8	8	8	7	7	7	4	3	3
France [2]	37	44	44	5	6	6	2	2	2	3	5	5	11	12	12	9	9	9	3	4	4
Austria [2]	39	43	43	8	10	10	2	1	1	4	6	6	5	7	7	8	9	9	5	4	4
Luxembourg [2]	39	43	42	11	11	11	6	8	7	4	4	4	6	6	6	5	6	6	3	5	4
Ireland [2]	32	39	40	8	12	13	2	1	1	2	2	2	3	4	4	5	8	8	9	9	9
United Kingdom [2]	35	38	39	13	10	11	2	5	4	2	3	3	4	3	4	3	6	6	5	5	5
Finland [3]	35	37	38	17	17	18	1	1	1	–	–	–	3	3	3	6	8	8	5	5	5
Germany [2]	36	38	38	11	11	11	2	2	2	5	6	6	7	7	7	5	6	6	4	3	3

Greece	25	35	37	2	5	5	1	1	1		5	5		5	5	5	6	6	6	7	9
Italy [2]	25	35	36	4	9		2	3		2	2	2	9	9	9	4	5	5	4	3	3
Canada	32	33	33	11	12	12	4	3	3	1	2	2	2	3	3	4	4	5	4	4	4
New Zealand	31	34	33	17	20	21	4	3	2	–	–	–	–	–	–	3	4	4	4	4	4
Switzerland	30	32	33	11	11	11	2	2	2	3	3	3	3	3	3	2	3	3	3	3	3
Portugal	25	31	32							3	3	3	5	5	6	3	4	7	7	9	8
Australia	28	31	31	12	14	15	3	3	3	–	–	–	–	–	–	2	2	2	5	6	6
Spain	20	29	30	3	7	5	1	2	2	2	2	2	8	9	9	3	4	5	2	4	4
United States	29	29	29	10	10	10	3	2	2	3	3	3	4	5	5	2	2	2	3	2	2
Japan	21	28	29	5	7	7	4	6	6	2	3	3	3	4	4	–	–	–	3	3	3
Turkey	21	20	23	7	5	6	1	2	3	1	1	1	1	2	2	–	5	5	8	2	2
OECD average [4]	33	37	38	11	12	12	2	3	3	2	3	3	5	5	5	4	6	6	5	5	5

Source: Revenue statistics of OECD member countries 1965–87, Paris 1988

A blank space = not available or non-existent, a dash = 0 or less than 0.5 per cent

Notes:

1 Countries ranked in order of 1986 total tax to GDP ratio.

2 Countries with a value added tax as at 31 December 1986.

3 Countries where receipts from employees' social security contributions on an income tax base are shown under personal income taxes.

4 Excluding Portugal for personal and corporation income taxes for all years and Greece (1975) for for all social security contributions where receipts cannot be broken down.

Table 5.2 Tax reform proposals in OECD countries in the 1980s
(a) Taxes on income and profits

Country	*Date*	*Review body or document*	*Type of proposals under consideration or introduced*
Ireland	1981	Commission on taxation	Single rate of tax to apply to a comprehensive income base and expenditure surcharge. Main proposals rejected.
New Zealand	1982	Task force on tax reform	Tax base widened and marginal rates substantially reduced in 1986.
Sweden	1983	Income tax reform commission	Proposals to cut substantially marginal rates implemented 1983–6.
Norway	1984	Royal Commission on income tax reforms	Proposals to widen the tax base, reduce rates schedule and index the system currently being examined.
United States	1986	President's tax proposals for fairness, growth and simplicity	Personal and corporate tax base widened and substantial reductions in the rates of tax.
Netherlands	1986	Direct tax reform commission	Amalgamation of personal income tax and employees' social security contributions under consideration.
United Kingdom	1986	Green Paper on the reform of the personal income tax	Proposals to reform the treatment of one- and two-earner couples being implemented.

Denmark	1986	Government review	Gradual separation of the taxation of earned and unearned income, and lowering of top marginal rate of tax agreed to in 1986.
Belgium	1986	Royal Commission on tax harmonisation and simplification	Proposals awaited.
Germany	1986	Tax reform proposals likely after 1987 elections	Base widening and rate reduction.

(b) General consumption taxes

Country	*Date*	*Review body or document*	*Type of proposals under consideration or introduced*
Japan	1980s	Several review bodies	The introduction of VAT has been examined at various times.
New Zealand	1982	Task force on tax reform	Proposals to introduce a VAT (goods and service tax) implemented in 1986.
United States	1984	Treasury's tax reform plan	VAT examined and rejected.
Australia	1985	Tax summit	Retail sales tax examined and rejected.
Turkey	1985	Government review	VAT proposed and introduced in 1985.
Canada	1986	Government review	A VAT ('business transfer tax') is under consideration.
Portugal	1986	Government review	VAT introduced on entry into the EC.
Spain	1986	Government review	VAT introduced on entry into the EC.
Greece	1987	Government review	VAT will be introduced in 1987 as part of entry measures into the EC.

has recently reduced marginal rates of personal income tax and widened the income tax base by removing, or reducing, certain tax expenditures.

In the Mediterranean countries (Greece, Portugal, Spain and Turkey) recent reforms have focused on the introduction of VAT, the general consumption tax required for membership of the European Community to which Greece, Portugal and Spain now belong. In each of these countries it is likely that VAT will become a major source of tax revenue. In Turkey the decision to introduce a VAT was influenced by a desire to achieve a more balanced tax structure and, in particular, to reduce the relatively high reliance on personal income taxes. In all of these countries, the move to a VAT has been accompanied by a revision of the personal income tax system.

The common theme of tax reform proposals in the Scandinavian countries (Denmark, Sweden and Norway) is the need to reduce marginal rates of income tax. During recent years each of these countries has either implemented or announced its intention of cutting the top schedule rates of income tax.

The tax reform debate in Ireland and the United Kingdom has focused on two issues: how to improve the neutrality of the personal and corporate income tax, and how to change the tax mix in favour of indirect taxes. Though in each country tax reform commissions (the Meade Committee in the United Kingdom and the O'Brien Commission in Ireland) have advocated an expenditure tax, in neither has this had any impact on the actual changes implemented. In the United Kingdom, the Chancellor announced in his 1984 budget that many tax incentives provided to companies would be eliminated over a three-year period, and that the rate of corporate tax would be cut from 52 to 35 per cent. In 1988 both countries substantially reduced the rates of personal income tax and in the UK there are now only two rates (25 per cent and 40 per cent).

In the United States the 1986 tax reform substantially cut the marginal rates of tax (there are now two rates, of 15 and 28 per cent, instead of 15 brackets with a top rate of 50 per cent), abolished a wide range of tax privileges (particularly those relating to retirement provisions), and cut the corporate rates from 46 to 34 per cent for large corporations.

A common theme of the reforms described above is the need for greater fiscal neutrality – the belief that a tax system should interfere as little as possible with economic behaviour – and an understandably but probably unrealistic desire to reduce the complexity of tax systems. Most proposals suggest a widening of the tax base, accompanied by a lowering of the rates. Many are revenue neutral, though all involve a redistribution of the tax burden. Some suggest increasing the reliance on indirect taxes.

Aside from changes in the overall trend and structure of taxation, another major influence on the environment within which local government operates is the trend to decentralise the expenditure and revenue functions of government. In all countries local authorities have broad land planning and infrastructure provision powers, and provide a wide range of local services. In the 1970s in Belgium, Denmark and the Netherlands, and more recently in Spain, France and Portugal, major measures of legislative and administrative decentralisation were introduced that tend to broaden the economic and social functions of local authorities. Very few countries (notably the United Kingdom) have escaped this trend. The transfer of power from central government has in some cases benefited regions, provinces and states. In the Netherlands, Spain and the United States it has been carried out in the name of the 'new federalism'.

The arguments in favour of decentralised government can be summarised briefly. A decentralised government may be better informed about the needs of individuals or communities, and more responsive to these needs. Local citizens/taxpayers will be able to express their preferences by voting for different tax/benefit packages at the local level. Households and firms can migrate to localities with the desired tax/benefit packages. The administrative efficiency in the provision of certain services may be improved.

However, decentralisation is not without cost. The administrative cost of providing certain services at the local rather than at the national level may be high, at least where there are economies of scale attached to a service. The operation of government services at the local level may also be more subject to corruption and may lead to distributional effects which national government considers undesirable.

The importance attached to these advantages and disadvantages will vary according to the type of services being considered. But it does seem that there is a growing consensus that decentralisation has helped to release the creative energies of local authorities, and it is noteworthy that decentralised economies have tended to perform better than highly centralised economies.

TRENDS IN FINANCING

Before looking at the taxes used by state and local government, it is helpful to review briefly the recent trends in overall national tax

Table 5.3 Revenues and grants received by local government as percentages of GDP, EC countries

	Tax revenue			Non-tax revenue			Grants			Total		
	1975	*1985*	*1986*	*1975*	*1985*	*1986*	*1975*	*1985*	*1986*	*1975*	*1985*	*1986*
Belgium	1.91	2.38	2.32		0.05			0.42		1.91	2.85	2.32
Denmark	12.31	13.77	13.82	3.09	3.17	3.14	15.57	14.35	13.01	30.97	31.29	29.96
France	2.79	3.80	3.84	0.01	0.01	0.01	0.03	0.03	0.03	2.83	3.84	3.88
Germany	3.25	3.23	3.17	0.31	0.33	0.32	0.28	0.25	0.24	3.84	3.81	3.74
Ireland	2.29	0.88	0.95	2.48	3.16[1]		8.31	11.05[1]		13.07	15.09	
Italy	0.22	0.80		0.39	1.49	1.66	5.05			5.66	2.29	
Luxembourg	4.95	5.00	4.96	0.66	0.67[1]		3.47	2.78[1]		9.08	8.45	
Netherlands	0.50	1.08	1.02	0.17	0.27	0.26	1.36	1.60	1.54	2.04	2.95	2.83
United Kingdom	3.90	3.89	4.21	3.43	2.61		7.35	6.06		14.68	12.56	
Greece	0.88	0.47	0.40	0.50			0.03			0.95	0.47	
Portugal	0.01	1.12	1.21							0.01	1.12	1.21
Spain	0.84	3.31	3.00	0.03	0.09[1]		0.10	0.05[1]		0.96	3.45	
Unweighted average	2.83	3.21	3.31	1.13	1.05	1.13	4.05	4.08	4.68	6.72	7.23	7.43

Source: Revenue Statistics of OECD Member countries 1965–87, Paris 1987

Note:

1 Ireland, Luxembourg and Spain figures are given for 1984.

Table 5.4 Revenues and grants received by local government as percentages of total tax revenue + non-tax revenue + grants, EC countries

	Tax revenue			*Non-tax revenue*			*Grants*		
	1975	*1985*	*1986*	*1975*	*1985*	*1986*	*1975*	*1985*	*1986*
Belgium		83.48			1.64			14.88	
Denmark	39.74	44.00	46.12	9.99	10.14	10.47	50.27	45.86	43.41
France	98.71	98.96	98.92	0.34	0.30	0.29	0.95	0.74	0.79
Germany	84.60	84.85	84.89	8.05	8.62	8.62	7.35	6.52	6.48
Ireland[1]	17.51	5.54		18.96	21.02		63.53	73.44	
Italy							89.21		
Luxembourg[1]	54.48	58.75		7.27	7.98		38.26	33.27	
Netherlands	24.71	36.50	36.16	8.55	9.05	9.25	66.74	54.45	54.59
United Kingdom	26.56	30.95		23.35	20.78		50.08	48.27	
Greece	92.04			5.21			2.75		
Portugal									
Spain[1]	87.38	96.83		2.71	2.04		9.91	1.13	
Unweighted average	58.41	59.98		9.38	9.06		37.91	30.95	

Source: Revenue Statistics of OECD Member countries 1965–87, Paris 1988

Note:

1 Ireland, Luxemburg and Spain figures are given for 1975, 1984, and 1986.

burdens, since these have been influential at the local level. The first three columns of Table 5.1 indicate what has been happening to the total tax burdens in OECD countries. Over the period 1965 to around 1975 most OECD countries had increased their tax levels quite rapidly. Moreover, with a few exceptions, countries could be identified by the following geographical groupings:

a high tax countries: northern Europe (e.g. Belgium, Denmark, Netherlands, Norway and Sweden)
b medium tax countries: OECD outside Europe (e.g. Australia, Canada, New Zealand and United States)
c low tax countries: southern Europe (e.g. Greece, Portugal, Spain and Turkey).

Over the last decade or so, this pattern has changed. While in some northern European countries total tax levels increased quite considerably, in others total tax yields became stable for many years, or even declined (Austria, Finland and Germany). Apart from Japan, the non-European OECD countries have scarcely increased tax levels over the last ten years, and tax yields have actually fallen in the United States. In contrast, the lowest taxed countries of southern Europe

Table 5.5 Attribution of tax revenues to sub-sectors of general government as percentages of total tax revenue, OECD countries

	Supranational			*Central government*			*State*			*Local*			*Social security*		
	1975	*1985*	*1986*	*1975*	*1985*	*1986*	*1975*	*1985*	*1986*	*1975*	*1985*	*1986*	*1975*	*1985*	*1986*
Federal countries															
Australia				79	81	81	16	16	16	4	4	4	–	–	–
Austria				52	49	49	11	13	13	12	11	11	25	27	27
Canada				48	41	42	33	36	35	10	9	9	10	13	14
Germany	1	1	1	34	32	31	22	22	22	9	9	8	33	37	37
Switzerland				27	29	30	24	23	22	20	17	16	29	32	32
United States				43	40	39	18	19	19	14	12	12	25	29	30
Unweighted average				47	45	45	21	21	21	11	10	10	20	23	23

Unitary countries															
Belgium	1	2	1	63	62	61				5	5	5	31	32	32
Denmark	1	–	1	69	69	70				30	28	27	1	2	2
Finland				60	60	61				27	26	26	14	14	14
France	1	2	2	50	46	46				8	9	9	41	43	43
Greece	–	1	1	69	62	66				4	1	1	27	35	32
Ireland	2	2	2	77	82	83				7	2	2	13	14	13
Italy	–	1		53	62	66				1	2		46	35	34
Japan				45	44	45				26	26	26	29	30	30
Luxembourg	1	1	1	58	63	63				13	12	12	29	25	25
Netherlands	2	1	1	59	52	54				1	2	2	38	44	42
New Zealand				92	94					8	6		–	–	–
Norway				51	60	57				22	18	19	27	22	24
Portugal				65	70	68				–	4	4	35	26	28
Spain				48	47	51				4	11	10	47	41	39
Sweden				51	54	56				29	30	28	20	16	16
Turkey					76	77					10	10		14	13
United Kingdom	1	1	1	71	71	70				11	10	11	17	18	18
Unweighted average[1]	1	1	1	61	62	57				13	13	12	26	24	24

Source: Revenue statistics of OECD member countries 1965–87, Paris 1988

Note:

1 Turkey and Greece are excluded.

have increased the total tax ratio considerably (save for Turkey, where there has been a large fall).

Table 5.1 gives also some indication of the difference between countries in their relative reliance on different sources of revenue and how this relative reliance has fluctuated between 1965 and 1984. In countries like Germany and Switzerland, most ratios are not far from the OECD average, and their movement over eighteen years has been relatively slight. At a less disaggregated level, however, it may be observed that in most countries there was a considerable increase in the income tax and/or social security ratio between 1965 and 1974, accompanied by a scarcely-changing consumption tax ratio. After the mid 1970s, however, growth in the personal income tax and social security ratios become sluggish in many countries, whereas consumption tax ratios tended to increase more and more. Thus the general trend away from consumption taxes to income and payroll taxes, which had in fact been occurring even since 1955, came gradually to a halt in the mid to late 1970s, and in some countries (e.g. Denmark, Finland, United Kingdom) the trend was reversed.

Turning to lower levels of government, four sources of finance are available: taxes, non-tax revenues, grants, and borrowing. The last of these sources of finance is not considered here, since in all countries the borrowing of local governments is strictly controlled by higher levels of government, and is generally limited to financing capital projects. Non-tax revenue covers all government revenue other than compulsory tax payments, grants and borrowing. Tables 5.3 and 5.4 show that, on average, taxes in the EC countries account for 60 per cent of total revenues (excluding loans), non-tax revenues for 9 per cent, and grants for 31 per cent. Tables 5.3 and 5.4 are limited to the twelve EC countries, because comparable data are not available for many of the non-EC countries. Over the last ten years the trend has been for the relative importance of taxes to increase and for that of non-tax revenues and grants to fall somewhat.

Table 5.5 provides an overview of the attribution of tax revenues to different levels of government in all OECD countries. It shows that in the federal countries, on average, 45 per cent of tax revenues accrue to central government, 21 per cent to state government, 10 per cent to local government and 23 per cent to social security funds. Over the last ten years, the tendency has been for the share of central government to fall, that of state and local governments to remain more or less unchanged, while the share of social security funds has significantly increased.

In unitary countries, on average, 63 per cent of tax revenues accrue to central government, 13 per cent to local government and 24 per cent to social security funds. The tendency has been for the share of central government to increase, while that of local government has remained stable.

Tables 5.6 and 5.7 show the relative importances of the main taxes used by state and local governments. In the eighteen unitary countries most local governments rely predominantly on one tax source – usually either income tax (six countries) or property tax (four countries). Over the last ten years, the tendency in federal countries has been to place less reliance on property and business taxes, a more or less unchanged reliance on corporate and sales taxes, and an increased reliance on income tax sources. In unitary countries the most noticeable trend has been to decrease the relative burden of the income tax and increase that of other local taxes, though property taxes have remained more or less unchanged.

The changing importance of the property tax is highlighted in Table 5.8, which shows that in 1985 property tax revenues amounted, on average, for 25 per cent of total tax revenues in unitary countries and 45 per cent in federal countries. Over the ten-year period covered by the table, the relative importance of the property tax has fallen in almost half of the countries, and sometimes significantly so. In the European context, this reduction is mainly explained by infrequent revaluations of the tax base and central government imposed system of tax reliefs.

THE INTERACTION BETWEEN CENTRAL AND LOCAL TAX SYSTEMS

This section examines the links between central and local tax systems. It first looks at the question of local fiscal autonomy and the ways in which central government can assign a tax base to local government, then it examines the extent of central government control over local taxes. Finally, it discusses why central government would wish to constrain the fiscal discretion of local government.

The issues of local autonomy and local accountability are closely linked, since one of the main reasons for giving local government a degree of fiscal discretion is to encourage local accountability. This, in turn, enables local electorates to influence the mix of local taxes and services, thereby promoting a more efficient allocation of resources and encouraging cost containment at the local level.

Table 5.6 Tax revenues of the main state and local taxes as percentages of GDP, OECD countries

	Personal income taxes			*Corporate income taxes*			*Payroll taxes*			*Taxes on property*			*Consumption taxes*			*Other*[1]		
	1975	1985	1986	1975	1985	1986	1975	1985	1986	1975	1985	1986	1975	1985	1986	1975	1985	1986
Federal countries																		
Australia																		
State	–	–	–	–	–	–	1.7	1.6	1.6	0.3	0.3	0.3	1.6	1.9	2.0	0.9	0.9	1.0
Local	–	–	–	–	–	–	–	–	–	1.2	1.1	1.1	–	–	–	–	–	–
Austria																		
State	1.7	2.8	2.8	0.1	0.2	0.2	–	0.3	0.3	–	–	–	2.1	2.2	2.1	0.1	0.2	0.2
Local	1.6	1.6	1.6	0.2	0.2	0.3	0.5	0.5	0.5	0.3	0.3	0.2	1.7	1.6	1.6	0.4	0.4	0.4
Canada																		
State	3.4	4.5	4.7	1.2	0.8	0.8	–	–	–	–	0.2	0.2	5.7	6.1	5.6	0.2	0.2	0.3
Local	–	–	–	–	–	–	–	–	–	2.7	2.5	2.5	0.1	–	–	0.4	0.6	0.6
Germany[2]																		
State	4.4	4.4	4.3	0.6	1.0	0.9	–	–	–	–	–	–	2.5	2.6	2.7	0.5	0.5	0.5
Local	1.9	2.2	2.1	0.4	0.5	0.4	0.3	–	–	0.4	0.4	0.4	–	–	–	0.3	0.2	0.2
Switzerland																		
State	4.5	4.7	4.7	1.0	0.8	0.9	–	–	–	–	–	–	0.6	0.6	0.5	1.0	1.1	1.1
Local	4.2	4.1	4.0	0.8	0.6	0.5	–	–	–	0.1	0.1	0.1	–	–	–	0.6	0.6	0.6
United States																		
State		1.6	1.6		0.5	0.4	–	–	–	0.1	0.1	0.1	3.4	3.3	3.2	1.8	0.1	0.1
Local		0.2	0.2		–	–	–	–	–	3.3	2.6	2.6	0.6	0.7	0.7	0.2	–	–
Unweighted average:																		
State	2.4	3.0	3.0	0.5	0.5	0.5	0.3	0.3	0.3	0.1	0.1	0.1	2.7	2.8	2.7	0.7	0.5	0.5
Local	1.3	1.3	1.3	0.2	0.2	0.2	0.1	0.1	0.1	1.3	1.2	1.2	0.4	0.4	0.4	0.3	0.3	0.3

Unitary countries																		
Belgium[2]	1.2	1.6	1.5	0.2	0.3	0.3	–	–	–	–	–	–	0.4	0.4	0.4	0.1	0.1	0.1
Denmark[2]	10.4	12.5	12.5	0.2	0.4	0.4	–	–	–	1.6	0.9	0.9	–	–	–	–	–	–
Finland	8.6	8.7	9.0	0.8	0.8	0.8	–	–	–	–	0.1	0.1	–	–	–	–	–	–
France[2]	0.6	0.6	0.6	–	–	–	0.1	0.2	0.2	0.5	1.0	1.0	0.2	0.5	0.5	1.3	1.5	1.5
Greece[2]	0.1	–	–	–	–	–	0.1	0.2	0.3	–	–	–	0.5	0.2	0.1	0.1	–	–
Ireland[2]	–	–	–	–	–	–	–	–	–	2.3	0.9	0.9	–	–	–	–	–	–
Italy[2]	0.1	0.1		0.1	0.1		–	–	–	–	–	–	–	0.3		–	0.3	
Japan	1.4	2.1	2.2	1.5	2.1	2.0	–	–	–	1.2	1.6	1.7	1.1	1.3	1.3	0.1	0.2	0.2
Luxembourg[2]	1.8	1.7	1.8	2.0	2.4	2.3	0.4	0.2	0.2	0.2	0.2	0.2	0.5	0.4	0.4	–	–	–
Netherlands[2]	0.1	–	–	–	–	–	–	–	–	0.3	0.8	0.8	0.2	0.3	0.3	–	–	–
New Zealand	–	–	–	–	–	–	–	–	–	2.1	1.9		0.3	0.1		–	–	–
Norway	8.7	7.1	7.7	0.6	0.6	0.7	–	–	–	0.2	0.2	0.2	–	–	0.1	0.6	0.6	0.6
Portugal							–	–	–	–	–	–	–	0.4	0.5	–	0.7	0.7
Spain	0.4	1.3	0.5	–	0.1	0.1	–	–	–	0.1	0.1	–	0.3	1.3	1.2	0.1	0.6	1.2
Sweden	11.7	15.0	15.1	1.0	0.2	–	–	–	–	–	–	–	–	–	–	–	–	–
Turkey		0.6	0.7		0.2	0.3	–	–	–					0.8	0.8		0.4	0.4
United Kingdom[2]	–	–	–	–	–	–	–	–	–	3.9	3.9	4.2	–	–	–	–	–	–
Unweighted average[3]	3.0	3.4	3.4	0.4	0.5	0.4	–	–	–	0.8	0.8	0.7	0.2	0.3	0.3	0.2	0.3	0.3

Source: Revenue statistics of OECD member countries 1965–87, Paris 1988

Notes:

1 Includes social security contributions attributable to local government (Belgium), to state and local governments (Austria), taxes on net wealth (Finland and Portugal) and some residual taxes mainly on business (Austria, Canada, Denmark, Germany, France, Greece, Italy, Netherlands, New Zealand, Norway).

2 Payments to the European Communities are excluded from these comparisons.

3 Turkey and Greece are excluded.

Table 5.7 Tax revenues of the main local taxes as percentage of total tax revenues of local government and state and local taxes, OECD countries

	Personal income taxes			*Corporate income taxes*			*Payroll taxes*			*Taxes on property*			*Consumption taxes*			*Other*[1]		
	1975	*1985*	*1986*	*1975*	*1985*	*1986*	*1975*	*1985*	*1986*	*1975*	*1985*	*1986*	*1975*	*1985*	*1986*	*1975*	*1985*	*1986*
Federal countries																		
Australia																		
State	–	–	–	–	–	–	38.4	35.0	33.3	6.2	6.2	6.3	36.0	40.6	40.2	19.4	18.3	20.2
Local	–	–	–	–	–	–	–	–	–	97.5	96.0	96.1	2.5	4.0	3.9	–	–	–
Austria																		
State	42.7	49.5	50.2	1.6	3.3	3.5	–	4.6	4.6	0.8	0.5	0.5	51.8	38.7	37.8	3.2	3.4	3.3
Local	33.8	34.4	34.7	5.1	5.0	5.5	11.5	11.0	11.0	6.1	5.6	5.4	34.8	34.9	34.5	8.8	9.1	8.9
Canada																		
State	32.4	37.8	40.6	11.2	7.0	6.8	–	–	–	0.5	1.9	1.9	54.1	51.2	48.5	1.8	2.0	2.2
Local	–	–	–	–	–	–	–	–	–	84.1	79.7	79.9	2.1	1.2	1.2	13.7	19.0	18.9
Germany[2]																		
State	55.2	52.0	51.7	7.5	11.3	10.9	–	–	–	–	–	–	31.1	31.3	31.8	6.2	5.5	5.6
Local	58.3	66.6	66.5	11.1	14.0	14.1	9.0	–	–	12.5	12.5	12.4	0.9	0.8	0.8	8.3	6.2	6.2
Switzerland																		
State	63.6	65.5	64.2	14.2	11.4	12.5	–	–	–	0.6	0.6	0.6	8.0	7.6	7.5	13.7	14.9	15.3
Local	73.2	76.7	76.5	13.4	10.4	10.5	–	–	–	2.2	2.0	2.0	0.3	0.3	0.3	10.9	10.6	10.7
United States																		
State		29.5	29.5		8.2	8.0	–	–	–	1.8	1.8	1.8	64.4	58.7	58.6	33.8	1.8	1.9
Local		4.8	4.7		1.1	1.2	–	–	–	81.9	74.2	74.0	13.7	19.9	20.1	4.3	–	–
Unweighted average:																		
State	32.3	39.0	39.4	5.7	6.9	7.0	6.4	6.6	6.3	1.6	1.8	1.8	40.9	38.0	37.4	13.0	7.6	8.1
Local	27.5	30.4	30.4	4.9	5.1	5.2	3.4	1.8	1.8	47.4	45.0	45.0	9.1	10.2	10.1	7.7	7.5	7.5

Unitary countries

Belgium[2]	60.6	65.9	66.2	12.3	12.4	11.6	–	–	–	–	–	–	20.4	15.9	16.3	6.8	5.8	5.9
Denmark[2]	84.8	90.9	90.3	1.6	2.6	2.7	–	–	–	13.2	6.4	6.8	0.3	0.2	0.1	0.1	–	–
Finland	91.4	90.5	90.5	8.3	8.5	8.5	–	–	–	–	0.9	0.9	0.2	0.1	0.1	–	–	–
France[2]	23.0	16.7	16.6	–	–	–	4.8	5.1	4.8	19.1	25.2	25.3	7.9	13.4	13.9	45.2	39.7	39.4
Greece[2]	11.0	9.5		–	–	–	16.3	40.8	73.4	2.7	4.6		60.6	40.2	26.6	9.4	4.7	
Ireland[2]	–	–	–	–	–	–	–	–	–	100.0	100.0	100.0	–	–	–	–	–	–
Italy[2]	48.0	16.0		32.0	10.7		–	–	–	17.5	–		2.5	33.3		–	40.1	
Japan	26.3	28.9	29.5	28.5	29.2	27.6	–	–	–	22.7	21.9	22.8	20.1	17.2	17.2	2.5	2.9	3.0
Luxembourg[2]	37.2	34.2	35.6	39.5	48.8	46.9	8.0	4.7	4.9	4.9	4.2	4.2	10.3	8.0	8.4	–	–	–
Netherlands[2]	15.4	–	–	–	–	–	–	–	–	54.2	75.2	74.3	30.4	24.8	25.7	–	–	–
New Zealand	–	–	–	–	–	–	–	–	–	89.1	93.0		10.9	7.0		–	–	–
Norway	86.3	83.4	82.9	5.7	6.8	7.2	–	–	–	1.9	2.5	2.6	–	0.5	0.7	6.2	6.8	6.6
Portugal							–	–	–	–	–	–	50.0	33.7	43.3	50.0	66.3	56.7
Spain	43.0	38.2		–	2.1	2.4	–	–	–	8.5	1.8	0.9	34.2	39.9	41.0	14.3	18.0	
Sweden	91.5	98.3	99.7	8.2	1.4	–	–	–	–	–	–	–	0.4	0.3	0.3	–	–	–
Turkey		30.6	31.5		11.8	14.2	–	–	–		0.7	–		38.7	36.9		18.3	17.5
United Kingdom[2]	–	–	–	–	–	–	–	–	–	100.0	100.0	100.0	–	–	–	–	–	–
Unweighted average[3]	40.5	37.5	39.3	9.1	8.2	7.1	0.9	0.7	0.6	28.7	28.7	22.5	12.5	12.9	11.1	8.3	12.0	10.1

Source: Revenue statistics of OECD member countries 1965–87, Paris 1988

Notes:

1 Includes social security contributions attributable to local government (Belgium), to state and local government (Austria), taxes on net wealth (Finland and Portugal) and some residual taxes mainly on business (Austria, Canada, Denmark, Germany, France, Greece, Italy, Netherlands, New Zealand, Norway).

2 Payments to the European Communities are excluded from these comparisons.

3 Turkey and Greece are excluded.

Table 5.8 Taxes on immovable property as percentages of total tax revenues of local or state and local government, OECD countries

	Taxes on individuals			*Taxes on enterprises*			*Total*		
	1975	*1985*	*1986*	*1975*	*1985*	*1986*	*1975*	*1985*	*1986*
Federal countries									
Australia									
State							6.2	6.2	6.3
Local							97.5	96.0	96.1
Austria									
State	0.8	0.5	0.5	–	–	–	0.8	0.5	0.5
Local	0.9	0.6	0.5	5.2	5.0	4.9	6.1	5.6	5.4
Canada									
State							0.5	1.9	1.9
Local							84.1	79.7	79.9
Germany									
State	–	–	–	–	–	–	–	–	–
Local	7.5	5.0	5.0	5.0	7.5	7.5	12.5	12.5	12.4
Switzerland									
State	0.6	0.6	0.6	–	–	–	0.6	0.6	0.6
Local	2.2	2.0	2.0	–	–	–	2.2	2.0	2.0
United States									
State							1.8	1.8	1.9
Local							81.9	74.2	74.0
Unweighted average:									
State	0.2	0.2	0.2				1.6	1.8	1.8
Local	1.8	1.3	1.3	1.7	2.1	2.1	47.4	45.0	45.0
Unitary countries									
Belgium	–	–	–	–	–	–	–	–	–
Denmark	–	–	–	13.2	6.4	6.8	13.2	6.4	6.8
Finland	–	0.6	0.6	–	0.3	0.3	–	0.9	0.9
France	12.5	16.9	16.9	6.5	8.3	8.3	19.1	25.2	25.3
Greece	–	–	–	2.7	4.8		2.7	4.8	
Ireland							100.0	100.0	100.0
Italy							17.5	–	
Japan							22.7	21.9	22.8
Luxembourg							4.9	4.2	4.2
Netherlands							54.2	75.2	74.3
New Zealand							89.1	93.0	
Norway		2.5	2.6			–	1.9	2.5	2.6
Portugal	–	–	–	–	–	–	–	–	–
Spain	8.5			–	–	–	8.5	1.8	0.9
Sweden	–	–	–	–	–	–	–	–	–
Turkey								0.7	–
UK	38.3	43.0	42.2	61.7	57.7	57.8	100.0	100.0	100.0
Unweighted average							25.5	25.7	24.1

A blank indicates that a breakdown between households and others is not available.
Source: Revenue statistics of OECD member countries 1965–87, Paris 1988

Local accountability requires that the revenue consequences of locally-determined expenditure increases should be passed on to local electorates either through taxation or user charges. This process would seem to be facilitated if local governments have their own tax resources and are able to fix their tax rates by reference to the level of public services asked for by their local electorates. On this basis, it has been argued that there is a case for relatively large local taxes to finance local government in relation to other sources of finance, such as grants, over which the local government authorities may have little or no control. It is for these reasons that in some countries (e.g. Denmark) the central government insists that local government levies a local tax and in some cases fixes a minimum as well as a maximum rate of tax.

However, arguments have been put against this point of view. On the one hand, it can be argued that the ideals of local autonomy and accountability conflict with other desiderata, such as horizontal equity, especially if equalisation is incomplete so that tax differences do not accurately reflect differences in services received. On the other hand, whether grants reduce autonomy is an issue which may be less clear-cut than is sometimes assumed. Also of relevance to these questions is the fact that locally-imposed fees and charges are visible sources of revenue, and their use may improve local autonomy and accountability.

Table 5.9 ranks the main sources of local government finance by their potential contribution to local autonomy. Own taxes and overlapping taxes are levies over which local authorities have some direct control. It is these taxes which provide a direct link between local spending and revenue decisions at the level of a particular unit of local government. Shared taxes cannot fulfil this role, since an increase in the expenditure of a particular unit of local government has no direct impact on the taxes paid within that local authority. Non-tax revenues are another source of revenue over which local authorities may have some direct control and which can contribute to local authority. Non-tax revenues are another source of revenue over which local authorities may have some direct control and which can contribute to local autonomy. Data available for the EC countries suggest that about a fifth of local expenditure is financed from own/overlapping taxes and, if non-tax revenues are included, this proportion rises to one-third. (These data are not the same as those reproduced in Table 5.7, since that table refers to the proportion of total revenue derived from different sources and no breakdown is provided between own taxes and shared taxes.) The position in individual countries, however, varies considerably.

Table 5.9 A ranking of sources of finance by the degree of fiscal autonomy that they would normally provide to local government

1	Own taxes:	Base and rate under local control.
2	Overlapping taxes:	Nationwide tax base, but rates under local control.
3	Non-tax revenues:	Local government is able to determine the fee to be charged.
4	Shared taxes:	Nationwide base and rates, but with local government able to influence either the proportion of revenues attributed to the local government sector or the amount that each unit of local government receives.
5	General purpose grants:	Local government share is fixed by central government (usually with a redistributive element), but local government is free to determine how the funds should be spent.
6	Specific grants:	The amount of the grant may be determined by central government or may depend upon the spending decisions of local government, but in either case central government specifies how the funds should be spent.

In practice, fiscal autonomy in the EC area tends to be constrained in Belgium, Greece, Ireland, Luxembourg, the Netherlands and, to a lesser extent, in Germany, whereas in Denmark, France, Spain and the United Kingdom, local authorities have a greater degree of fiscal discretion. Nevertheless, where local government has responsibility for a wide range of public services and where grants take the form of general-purpose grants which leave local authorities some discretion over the allocation of these monies, local autonomy may not be quite as constrained as is suggested by these comparisons.

A useful method to illustrate the interaction between central and local government tax systems is to examine the way in which local income and property taxes operate since these are, in practice, the two major taxes used by local government.

State and local income taxes may take one of four forms:

a Tax-sharing arrangements: under such arrangements lower levels of government are automatically attributed a fixed percentage of the overall income tax receipts within a country. The division of these receipts between the individual units of local or state governments is usually determined by the division of the tax base between these units. Such tax-sharing arrangements exist in Austria, Germany, Luxembourg and Spain.

b Separate tax rates: state and local governments have the right to decide upon the rate of tax that they levy on the taxable income or tax paid as determined under the central government income tax system. These systems are sometimes referred to as 'piggy-backing'. This is the system operating in Belgium, Canada (except Quebec) and Denmark.

c Separate rate and allowance structures: although the income subject to tax is for the most part the same for central and local income taxation, the tax reliefs available to local taxpayers are not the same as those available under the central government income tax. Each unit of local government applies its chosen tax rate (or rates) to the taxable income so determined. These systems are used in Finland, Japan and Sweden.

d Separate tax systems: under these systems, subordinate levels of governments determine the base and the rate for income tax. In practice, however, the base is usually similar to that of the central government income tax. Separate tax systems are used in Switzerland, the United States and the Canadian province of Quebec.

The main characteristic of state and local income taxes are described in Table 5.10, though tax-sharing arrangements are not considered further in that table. As regards the tax base, the main distinction is between those countries where the tax base corresponds to the taxable income or tax paid to central government and those where it does not.

The main difference between countries as regards the rate schedule is that in the majority of countries lower levels of government use a single rate schedule, which usually varies throughout the country, while in three countries (Japan, Switzerland and the United States) there exist progressive schedules at the state and local level.

The last column of the table shows that in Japan, Switzerland and the United States subordinate levels of government are responsible for the assessment and the collection of income taxes, whereas in Belgium, Canada, Finland, Norway and Sweden they are both

Table 5.10 State and local government personal income taxes, OECD countries, 1983

Country	*Tax base*	*Rate schedule used (%)*		*Tax credits available under the state and local income tax*	*Deductibility against central government income tax*	*Allocation of tax base between localities (earned income)*	*Responsibility for assessment and collection*
		Single rate[1]	*Separate progressive rate schedule*				
Belgium	Central government income tax paid	6–8 (Av)		None	No	Residence	Central government
Canada (excluding Quebec)[2]	Central government tax paid before allowance for general tax credits	38.5–59.0 (Av=47)		Some provinces provide tax credits for low income groups	No	Residence	Central government
Denmark	Central government taxable income	20.2–33.5 (Av=27.1)		None	No	Residence	Central government for collection and local for assessment
Finland	Central government tax base and separate tax relief structure	14–18.5 (Av=15.9)		Yes	No	Residence	Central government

Japan	Central government tax base separate tax relief structure		4 to 18 + fixed amount	Yes	No[3]	Residence	Local government
Norway	Central government taxable income (minus dividend deduction)	23		None[4]	No	Residence	Central government
Sweden	Central government tax base and separate tax relief structure	26.0–33.7 (Av=30.2)		None	No[3]	Residence	Central government
Switzerland	Separate tax base in each canton		5 to 34[5]	Varies	No	Residence	Cantons
United States	Separate tax base in most states		2 to 14[6]	Yes in some States	Yes	Residence	States

Notes:
1 Minimum and maximum rates used.
2 Quebec operates a separate provincial income tax system.
3 A ceiling applies to the effective rate of central and local government income taxes. Any excess is refunded under the local income tax in Japan.
4 The same tax credits as for central government income tax are given for dependants and special bank savings accounts.
5 Zurich.
6 New York.

Table 5.11 Administrative responsibilities of different levels of governments for property taxes, OECD countries

Country	*Tax*	*Beneficiary government*	*Valuations*	*Assessments*	*Collection*
Australia[1]					
	Land tax	State government	State government	State government	State government
	Rates	State government and local authorities	State government	Local authorities	Local authorities
Denmark					
	Land tax	Municipalities and counties	Central government	Municipalities and counties	Municipalities and counties
	Service tax		Central government		
France					
	Land and Land and building taxes	Local authorities	Central government	Central government	Central government
	Property Tax	Local authorities	Central government	Central government	Central government
Germany					
	Real property tax (*Grundsteuer*)	Local authorities[2]	Central government	Local authorities[2,3]	Local authorities[2,3]
Japan					
	Fixed assets tax	Local authorities[2]	Local authorities[2]	Local authorities[2]	Local authorities[2]
	City planning tax	Local authorities[2]	Local authorities[2]	Local authorities[2]	Local authorities[2]
	Special land-holding tax	Local authorities[2]	Individuals	Individuals	Local authorities[2]
Netherlands					
	Municipal tax	Local authorities[2]	Local authorities	Central government and local authorities	Central government
	Contributions to polder boards	Local authorities[4]	Local authorities[4]	Local authorities[4]	Local authorities[4]

New Zealand					
	Land tax	Central government	Central government	Central government	Central government
	Rates	Local authorities	Central government	Local authorities	Local authorities
Spain					
	Rural land tax	Local authorities	Joint agencies[5]	Joint agencies[5]	Joint agencies[5]
	Urban land tax	Local authorities	Joint agencies[5]	Joint agencies[5]	Joint agencies[5]
Sweden					
	Municipal guarantee tax	Local authorities	Central government	Central government	Central government
Turkey					
	Immovable property tax	Central government	Central government	Central government	Central government
United Kingdom					
	Rates	Local authorities[6]	Central government[7]	Local authorities	Local authorities[8]
United States[9]					
	Property tax	State government and local authorities	State government and local authorities	State government and local authorities	State government and local authorities

Notes:
1 State of New South Wales
2 Municipalities
3 Assessment and collection in Hamburg and Berlin are central government responsibilities
4 Polder boards
5 Representing central government and local authorities
6 And central government in Northern Ireland
7 Except in Scotland
8 Except in Northern Ireland
9 State of Wisconsin

assessed and collected by the central government. In Denmark they are assessed by local government but collected by the central government.

Taxes on immovable property are the second most important source of tax revenues for local governments – see Table 5.7. A number of reasons explain the use of this tax by local government: the base of the tax is immovable property that cannot leave the locality; the rate of tax can be varied as between tax authorities without a serious risk of the migration of capital and residents; the tax can sometimes be seen as the application of the benefit principle of taxation to financing local services; it is clear which local government is entitled to tax each property; the yield is relatively predictable; and the tax is easy to administer.

Although property taxes are predominantly local taxes, local governments do not generally have complete discretion over the tax base and the rate of tax, even where they are responsible for the assessment and collection of the tax. Central governments may specify the valuation procedure to be used throughout the country; they may establish the frequency of valuation; they tend to set limits on the tax rate than can be levied; and they generally specify a number of concessions or reliefs that must be provided. Three issues arise in this relationship between central and local government: first, what is the general distribution of administrative responsibilities; secondly, what are the arrangements for coordinating valuations; and thirdly what degree of discretion do state and local authorities have over the tax base and the tax rate.

The distribution of administrative responsibilities for property taxes is set out in Table 5.11. Although most of these taxes accrue to state or local governments, the central government is usually involved in their administration; the exceptions are Australia, Japan and the United States. Even where the central government is not involved in the administration of these taxes, it does not necessarily follow that the beneficiary government has complete responsibility.

In some cases, for example, the beneficiaries are local authorities which are the lower of two tiers of non-central government and which have some administration done for them by the upper tier. Also, there are usually various devices to coordinate valuation procedures where these are the responsibility of state and local authorities.

The valuation of property tax bases is usually the responsibility of central government and state authorities (see Table 5.11). Central governments may maintain responsibility for valuation because the base of the property tax may be related to the base of other taxes.

For example, in Germany, the latest revaluations are used to calculate the tax bases for the net wealth tax, the inheritance tax, the trade tax and the taxation of the presumed rental income in the case of the owner-occupied house.

This coordination of the valuations of immovable property which enter into the assessment of different taxes is perhaps an approach that should be considered by any country which is reviewing its tax system. Having one valuation for land and building for the purpose of property taxes, death taxes, capital transfer taxes and the income tax simplifies tax administration, avoids inconsistent valuations of the same property, reduces taxpayer complaints and reduces compliance costs. Although the investment required in a centralised computerised valuation system is large, the long-run return is also high.

One of the major issues in the relationship between different levels of government in the property tax area is local authority discretion over the tax base and over tax rates. In the unitary countries, local discretion over the tax base exists only in the Netherlands and New Zealand, but in each case it is limited to a choice of two or three possible tax bases. In each country, a local authority must use the chosen base for all properties in its area.

Local authorities frequently have some discretion over their tax rates. Thus there are no specific limitations on the municipal guarantee tax in Sweden, there were none over rates in the United Kingdom (although rates could be 'capped') and there are rarely any over property taxes in the United States. In many countries, however, there are limitations on the power to vary tax rates. Local authorities may require prior approval of central government for rate increases, or they may be limited by the rate of inflation.

The last two columns of Table 5.11 show that local authorities are usually responsible for the assessment and collection of property taxes. Nevertheless, as was pointed out above, the actual valuation of the property is usually in the hands of central government.

To summarise, almost all local authorities are subject to limitations on the choice of the tax base for a local income or property tax and many are also subject to limitations on the determination of the rates of these taxes. Even in countries like Denmark, where local authorities are free to determine the rate of local income tax, there may, nevertheless, be restraints which arise from the fear of large tax rate differentials promoting a movement of labour and capital from high-tax to low-tax jurisdictions. And few local authorities can afford to ignore entirely these tax competition aspects. Local authorities might also feel constrained in the determination of their tax rates if higher rates were to affect adversely grant receipts, a situation which existed in the United Kingdom. Similarly, insofar as tax revenues from a particular source have to be used to finance a particular type of expenditure (e.g. special property taxes used to finance refuse collection), this also limits the autonomy of local government.

Various reasons have been suggested for these limitations:

a National governments may prefer to give priority to controlling the growth of the public sector, or to avoid any conflicts with macro-economic goals.
b Tax rate increases may enter into published price indices.
c National governments may wish to prevent the creation of local tax havens and other forms of taxpayer segregation regarded as undesirable as a matter of national or regional policy.
d A local group which is unable to get its point of view accepted (for example, it may prefer a generally lower level of local services and local taxes) may associate with other similarly-disposed groups and complain to a higher level of government. Their combined pressure can lead to limits being imposed by the higher level of government.
e Central government may maintain the right to determine the base for a local tax where the same base is used for a national tax.
f Central government may consider it inappropriate that local government should become involved in redistribution issues.

It is beyond the scope of this note to assess the validity of these arguments. It is worth noting, however, that local autonomy is only one criterion by which to judge the alternative revenue sources of local government. Other criteria include long-term stability and predictability (e.g. a shared tax where the share is specified in the national constitution), ease of administration (a local authority may be prepared to give up a part of its freedom in return for central government taking over the administration of a tax) and visibility (local accountability requires taxes which are highly visible and which affect a large part of the local population).

CURRENT TRENDS IN THE USE OF PROPERTY TAXES

A number of European countries have recently reviewed the role of the property tax in financing local government. In some cases, this has been in the context of a policy to decentralise government expenditures and revenues. In other cases, it has been part of a wider review of local government finance. Some governments have decided to reinforce the role of property taxes whilst others have eliminated them. This section briefly reviews these trends.

Table 5.8 provides an overview of property tax yields during the last ten years. In most countries, the relative yields for these taxes have declined, though in some (e.g. the Netherlands and New Zealand) they have increased. There has also been a tendency to shift the burden from households to businesses.

A number of European countries have recently reviewed their methods of financing local governments and concluded that property taxes should be eliminated or substantially reduced. Thus, the United Kingdom has replaced the local property tax on domestic property by a poll tax which takes the form of a levy for each adult. A major motive behind this decision was to increase local accountability by making a larger number of local residents participate directly in the financing of local services.

Ireland abandoned its tax on domestic property in 1978, mainly because of criticisms of the fairness of the tax. Rural areas contributed very little, and valuations were very much out of date – the last full-scale valuation having taken place in 1850! Nevertheless, the need for a viable local tax source led the Government to introduce in 1983 a new residential property tax which took the form of a tax on imputed income from residential property. A major review of local finance is currently underview.

Some of the Swiss cantons (e.g. Zurich) decided in the early 1980s to abolish the property tax. The main reasons given were that these taxes were very costly to administer in relation to the yield, which tended to be small in comparison to other cantonal taxes.

It is of interest to note that countries where property taxes have been abandoned are usually countries which have not achieved regular revaluations of property values.

A second group of countries has decided to introduce new property taxes, or substantially to modify existing taxes on immovable property. In almost all cases, this has been part of a policy of devolution. Thus Spain has now completed its goal of decentralising many expenditure and revenue functions to newly-established regional governments. As part of this process, the methods of valuing properties were reviewed and local authorities were given greater autonomy over the tax rate. Regional governments were given a share of VAT and an attempt was made to provide local authorities with a share of income taxes. Portugal has also reviewed its local finance system, and it appears that a modernised system of property taxation will become the main source of financing local government there. The new tax will be based upon the capital value of properties determined on the basis of updated values. Greece is also in the process of decentralising and raising existing taxes on property.

6 How far is the poll tax a 'community charge'?

The implications of service usage evidence

Glen Bramley, Gordon Hamilton, Julian Le Grand and William Low

INTRODUCTION

A new system for financing local government has been introduced in Britain, from 1989 in Scotland and from 1990 in England and Wales. The centrepiece of this new system is an adult poll tax, officially termed the Community Charge. The overall thrust of the reform has been portrayed as being concerned with improving the financial accountability of local authorities to their electorates, although the reform was clearly also directed at reducing local public expenditure and at fulfilling a long-standing obligation to abolish domestic rates. As the official name of the new tax implies, the Government has quite explicitly attempted to set up a tax which resembles a charge for services, so that tax liabilities relate to the use and benefit derived from services, rather than ability to pay. This reflects the Government's view on the primary role of local government as a service provider, rather than an agency engaged in redistribution or economic management. Yet the equation of the poll tax with the notion of a charge or, more appropriately, a 'benefit tax', is based wholly on assertion, without any evidence about the actual usage or benefits of local authority services.

This paper sets out to assess this crucial element of the argument. It utilises evidence from a unique new survey of usage of most of the services provided by a major local authority, Cheshire County Council, to examine critically the relationship between service usage and tax liabilities across the income and socio-economic spectrum. Much interesting detail emerges about the very different patterns of usage of different services, but in addition some robust generalisations can be made which can be related to a wider set of insights into the distribution of the benefits of welfare and other public spending. The evidence does not support the view that service usage and benefits are evenly distributed across the population. Apart from the variations associated with demographic structure, which we would expect, there are also clearly systematic variations across the social and economic spectrum. Far from favouring the less well off, as some might assume, the overall distribution favours the better off. Thus the case for a poll tax is significantly weakened. Rates (the local property tax which the poll tax replaced) do not match benefits very closely either, but on at least some comparisons they come closer to being a benefit tax than the adult poll tax.

We first examine the arguments for the reform proposals developed in the Green Paper *Paying for Local Government* (Department of the Environment, 1986), drawing out the centrality of the benefit tax notion, and relating this to the theoretical literature on local government finance. We show that while there are some grounds for a benefit tax at local level, at least for some services, there is a crucial missing link in the argument, namely hard evidence on who actually benefits. We refer briefly to other issues raised by the reform but discussed more adequately elsewhere.

The Cheshire survey is then introduced with a brief description of its aims, sample, questionnaire and response. For each household, the survey identified units of usage of a large number of specific services provided by the County Council, accounting for most of the authority's net expenditure. Aggregate expenditure and service provision data were used to cost these units and thereby enable a cost-based value of usage to be calculated for households. We also discuss here the representativeness of Cheshire for local government as a whole.

We then discuss the choices of various groups for comparison and some of the methodological issues raised, particularly in relation to the crucial issue of household structure. We go on to discuss how alternative local tax liabilities may be calculated for comparison, including the issue of rebates.

In discussing the results we describe first some of the patterns at individual service level, before considering the picture for services as a whole relative to tax shares. The main comparisons are made across income groups, socio-economic groups, and housing tenure. The conclusions then draw out implications for the legitimacy of the poll tax in local government finance, and go on to indicate some issues concerning the distribution of local public services for further examination.

THE BENEFIT TAX PRINCIPLE

The Green Paper which introduced the poll tax reform made clear at a number of points that an important part of the case for reform was the desirability of relating payment for local services to the use made of them. As we shall see below, this is referred to in public finance as the 'benefit principle' of taxation. In arguing that domestic rates were unsatisfactory in promoting local accountability, the Green Paper suggested that:

> Domestic rates are paid by a minority of local electors, and vary in a way that now has little or no regard to the use made of local authority services. The burden of rates is carried on too few shoulders.
>
> (Department of the Environment, 1986, vii)

It went on to amplify the point:

> Domestic rates have many technical advantages. But they do not take any account of the composition of households or their consumption of local government services. This was less relevant in the past, when local government was responsible for services such as gas, electricity and water, where the basic provision was related to property ownership. But today most local authority services are provided for people, rather than property.
>
> (Department of the Environment, 1986, p.6)

The view of local government as a service-providing agency, and the inference that it should be financed by a benefit tax, is most apparent when the authors of the Green Paper reject the obvious alternative to rates, a local income tax:

> The third objection to a local income tax is rather different – that income tax is not an appropriate tax for local authorities. There is a broad distinction to be drawn between the roles of central Government and local authorities. Local authorities' essential role is to provide services – some 'beneficial', some 'redistributive'. Local councillors are judged on their performance in delivering these services. . . . The ideal local tax should fit in with local authorities' role as a service provider and promote the efficient provision of services to the levels desired by most members of the community. That argues in favour of a form of taxation which has at least some of the characteristics of a charge. It argues against a redistributive tax.
>
> (Department of the Environment, 1986, p.24)

It is clear from these quotations and other parts of the same document that the Government positively sought a benefit tax in its local finance reform. The reform had a number of other important concerns which should not be forgotten, particularly:

a to promote accountability and financial restraint by widening the tax base;
b to further the same ends by nationalising the non-domestic rate and fixing grants in such a way that the full marginal cost of local budgetary decisions should falls on residents/voters; and
c to redress the perceived 'unfairness' of domestic rates.

These issues were more than adequately debated in the literature responding to the Green Paper since its publication (see, for example: Bramley, 1987; Smith, 1988; Jackman, 1986; and Association of Metropolitan Authorities, 1986). As the debate proceeded, other issues received greater prominence: the costs and difficulties of collecting the poll tax; the implications for civil liberties; the distributional effects on particular groups or areas; the scope of rebates; and weaknesses of accountability associated with the grant system, business rating, and central controls. We do not deal further with these important issues here, but rather concentrate on the key notion of the poll tax as a benefit tax, an issue which has received little theoretical and virtually no empirical attention. What the literature on the other issues just mentioned points to is that the Government was on shaky ground with most of its other arguments: the reform package weakens local accountability in some ways as it strengthens it in others, it is manifestly regressive, it is costly and disruptive, and it is unpopular. If it can be shown that the poll tax does not even measure up as a benefit tax, its last remaining prop of legitimacy is removed.

What is the case in theory for a benefit tax at local level? A benefit tax can be seen to promote both a particular version of equity and also the goal of economic efficiency. In their classic text on public finance, Musgrave and Musgrave (1980, p.238) suggest that the benefit principle is first and foremost an interpretation of *equity*. Where an individual's tax equates roughly with the cost (or value) of services received by that individual, there is an obvious sense in which fairness is being achieved. The combination of services and taxes is distributionally neutral; individuals themselves are likely to perceive the tax as fair.

The alternative general principle of taxation is of course the 'ability to pay' principle, one which is far more familiar and taken for granted in the contemporary world. Here tax is determined by some measure of ability – income, wealth, property – without reference to the nature or distribution of the services or benefits financed thereby. Equity is judged with reference to one side of the account only. The rationale for this principle may be that the services financed are intentionally or inherently redistributive (e.g. social security) or else that the services are very complex and any attempt to assign benefits is fraught with difficulty.

Foster, Jackman and Perlman (1980) in their monumental work on local government finance utilised the distinction between 'beneficial' and 'redistributive' services, and it is significant that these terms were picked up in the Green Paper, as we have seen. Beneficial services are primarily those which are 'public goods' in the economic sense (Head, 1974), that is non-excludable and/or non-rival in consumption, plus any other local services whose provision is not primarily motivated by redistribution (Foster *et al.* 1980, p.41). Redistributive services are, by definition, the remainder.

This simple method of categorising services is a useful analytical device. In relation to local taxation, it leads to the view that beneficial services should be financed by benefit-type local taxes, insofar as they cannot be funded directly from user charges. The latter are unlikely to be the main method of finance, since it is by definition impractical or inefficient to charge for public goods and since, implicitly within this economic paradigm, non-public goods would be most efficiently provided in the market rather than by local government. Redistributive services at local level raise more problems, and there is a line of argument going back to Stigler (1957) and echoed by Musgrave and Musgrave that local government is an inappropriate locus for significant redistributive activity. Again, we find hints of this in the Government's arguments in the Green Paper. Foster *et al.* (1980, pp.44–5) suggest that economic logic leads to the view that redistributive service levels should be centrally determined and centrally financed. However, recognising other political and administrative arguments for local control of some of these services they suggest that an acceptable second-best solution would involve local taxes levied on the ability-to-pay principle, combined with equalisation grants (see also King, 1984, pp.147–54).

One difficulty that we have with this model of local government is that the distinction between beneficial and redistributive is too simple. Typical modern services are complex and arguably incorporate a number of features, such as externalities (partial publicness) and notions of minimum standards (an aspect of redistribution), simultaneously. How, to take the obvious example, does one categorise education, the most important local service? It is clearly both difficult and contentious to assign motives to the provision of any services. If local government services are generally mixed in character, this theory would suggest that local government should perhaps be financed by a combination of perhaps two taxes, where one relates more to one principle and the other more to the other (plus equalisation grants).

We stated earlier that, as well as equity, benefit taxes can also promote economic efficiency. There are at least three mechanisms which may be at work here. First, benefit taxes are often assumed to be what economists call 'lump-sum' taxes, which do not affect the price of labour or any other factors or goods, unlike, say, income taxes which are argued to have incentive effects and hence overall efficiency costs. Secondly, benefit taxes are more likely to promote local budgetary decisions which are allocatively efficient. If each user pays a tax related to the cost of services consumed, then it is more likely that the criterion of efficiency for public goods – that the sum of the marginal benefits equals the marginal cost – will be fulfilled. Indeed, with a perfect benefit tax it is possible to conceive of an idealised Pareto-efficient decision being reached by consensus. Even if local democratic processes are less perfect than this, the tendency to efficiency is likely to be greater than in situations where there is a wide divergence between marginal tax bills and benefits. The Government of course draws particular attention to the groups of people who, especially prior to recent social security changes, paid a zero marginal tax contribution.

Thirdly, it can be argued that benefit taxes can promote efficiency in relation to local public goods by an alternative mechanism, that of voting with one's feet (Foster *et al.* 1980, pp.220 and 233). Different localities present different packages of services with different tax prices, and consumers choose their favoured option. This model, which derives from Tiebout (1956), is controversial for a number of reasons. It assumes that there are lots of local authorities and that migration into homogeneous communities is feasible and creates no costs for individuals or societies; Foster *et al.* concede that it 'offends against common perceptions of equity'. This model can be rehearsed as an alternative to, or argument against, the system of equalisation grants, as discussed in King (1984, pp.147–54), but this goes beyond the scope of this paper. On the whole we do not find this model plausible for United Kingdom conditions. However, it has been implicitly appealed to in certain ministerial statements arguing against local income tax, where it was suggested that such a system would encourage migration by high income groups away from areas like inner cities. The belief that this problem is associated with local income tax rather than with the poll tax assumes that the poll tax acts as a perfect benefit tax. If, as we go on to show, the benefits of services are not uniform, but rather systematically favour the better-off, then the poll tax might also be accused of creating incentives to migrate by causing a systematic divergence between taxes and benefits.

Rates as a property tax were traditionally seen as a benefit tax. Basic public services could be seen as the protection of property; specific improvements (e.g. to streets or drainage) could be reflected in rating assessments; and the general level of and access to local services would be reflected in property values (Musgrave and Musgrave, 1980, p.470). But the general view of economists now, strongly expressed by Foster *et al.* (1980, pp.153–7), is that with the modern range of local services, and particularly with the dominance in the budget of education, rates are no longer a good proxy for benefits. This view is not usually supported with any specific evidence.

One of the quotations from the Green Paper given above indicates that the Government had taken on board the notion that local government services were once strongly related to property but no longer are to the same extent. An important alternative reform proposal, that of CIPFA (Hale *et al.*, 1985), envisaged a division of local services into property-based and people-based services and a corresponding dual local taxation structure using rates and a local income tax. As Jackman (1986) pointed out when reviewing these proposals, no evidence on the actual distribution of service benefits was put forward with this proposal.

Most of the recent debate over rates focused on the ability-to-pay principle, rather than the benefit principle. The history of rating indicates that this tax has always been as much to do with ability to pay as with benefits (Foster *et al.*, 1980). However, the Government stressed that rates are not a good proxy for ability to pay in terms of income (Department of the Environment, 1986, pp.20–1).

There is a further complication to be noted in the concept of a benefit tax. Reviewing an earlier literature, King (1984, pp.147–54) suggests that there are two distinct kinds of benefit tax. The first attempts to measure the consumer's demand price or value, while the second estimates the cost of the service used. The former may be more appropriate from an equity point of view, the latter from an efficiency one. More practically, the second is more likely to be capable of measurement; getting consumers to reveal their true preferences for public goods is one of the fundamental economic problems of the public sector. In this study we follow the second approach, assigning to households a value of services used based on cost.

It is clear, though, that there will be some services, those that are pure public goods like police and town planning, that are difficult or impossible to assign meaningfully to individual consumers. Any allocation of these is likely to be arbitrary.

It is worth bearing in mind the alternative, demand-based approach to valuing services, because it provides one notional way of handling pure public goods and because it has distributional implications. These may be illustrated by a simple diagram such as Figure 6.1, which shows the familiar downward-sloping demand curves. Most normal goods or services exhibit the tendency for people with more income to demand more of them. This is shown on the diagram by the demand schedule moving to the north-east as income increases. Thus, in Figure 6.1 D_1 is the demand of a lower-income household, and D_2 is that of a higher-income household. In a normal market for private goods the result would be that the second group would consume more, say X_2 rather than X_1, at the same price (in this case V_1). In the case of a local public good, everyone in the locality is forced to consume the same amount, in this instance X_1; what differs between the income groups now is the 'price', or marginal value (Culyer, 1980), they put on the same quantity. The higher income group value the same service more highly; the difference is between V_1 and V_2 in terms of marginal value, or the area of OX_1 times (V_2-V_1) in terms of the economic concept of welfare, known as 'consumer's surplus'. This kind of analysis would apply to public goods and also to other services provided in equal rationed quantities to all eligible individuals (e.g. education up to the minimum school-leaving age). What it shows is that if we chose to shift from a cost-based to a demand-based benefit tax, either for all services or for the category of pure public goods for which units of usage cannot be defined, we would tend to find a systematic positive relationship between benefits and income.

To sum up this discussion, the Government argued for a benefit type of tax for local government, rather than a tax based on ability to pay, and asserted (without evidence) that a uniform tax on adults would correspond better to the distribution of service benefits than the main alternatives. Local public finance theory provides some support for the use of a benefit tax, although the case is not overwhelming, given the nature of services provided in practice by contemporary British local government. Our argument is that the evidence on the

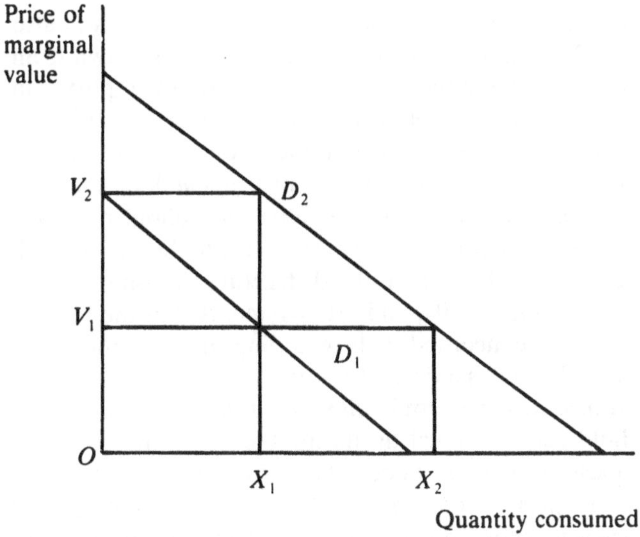

Figure 6.1 Demand and value for two income levels

distribution of service benefits should be examined; this evidence is likely to undermine the assumption that a flat-rate poll tax is a good proxy for benefits, and may rather suggest a convergence in practice between the benefit and ability-to-pay principles.

THE CHESHIRE STUDY

In 1986–7 the Research and Intelligence Unit of Cheshire County Council carried out a major household survey designed to give a detailed picture of the distribution of county council services across different households. Three of the authors of this paper were involved with this study in different ways. The study was aimed at providing detailed information for local service and budgetary planning purposes; but as a by-product it is possible to use it to address more general issues, both those relating to local government finance considered here, and wider issues about the role and distribution of public services in general. Although there have been a number of local authority sponsored opinion surveys, so far as we are aware this particular large-scale and comprehensive attempt to measure service usage through household interviews is unique in Britain.

The survey involved interviewing a random sample of households throughout Cheshire, and the analysis reported here is based on the response of 2,170 households covered in the first main phase of the survey. Later phases increased the random sample to 3,474 and also covered a further 2,400 households in enhanced samples drawn from service records for selected minority services. The results reported in this paper relate only to the first phase core sample. The responses can be shown to be broadly representative of households in Cheshire.

In addition to the main household questionnaire schedule, separate schedules were completed for each individual household member, subdivided by whether over or under 16 and whether at school. Questions were asked on basic household structure, housing tenure, employment and income details, and rate payments, but the bulk of the questionnaire was concerned with recording in detail the usage made of County Council services. In some cases a simple direct question was sufficient, for example 'how often did you or members of your household use a Council tip during the last year?' In other cases, several questions would be needed to get to a measure of usage – for instance in respect of roads or social workers. The time period over which usage was recorded varied as seemed appropriate, but was reduced for the purposes of analysis to an annual rate.

For each of twenty-five specific sub-services a unit of usage was defined, as shown in Table 6.1. For waste tips, for example, this would be visits per year; for road use it would be annual car mileage. There is obviously a degree of arbitrariness and simplification about this procedure; each sub-service was allocated wholly to one type of usage unit, so shared usage was discounted. No account was taken of 'externalities', that is of benefits (or costs) to people other than the direct users, who might or might not be Cheshire residents. While this was quite an important issue theoretically, it went beyond the practical scope of the research (see Le Grand, 1987, for further discussion).

As a separate exercise, the Cheshire County budget was divided into the same set of sub-service categories. As Table 6.1 shows, those sub-services for which individual usage could be meaningfully measured, and which were therefore covered in the survey, accounted for about 70 per cent of expenditure. (It is *net* expenditure which is used here. Charges are only significant for a few county services.) The total number of service units provided in Cheshire in the year for each sub-service was estimated, either using independent service records or using grossed-up survey figures. Dividing total expenditure by total usage units gave a 'cost per unit' for each sub-service. It is this figure that we used to provide a value weighting for each sub-service when aggregating up each household's usage across all the County Council services. At the end of the process, we had for each respondent household an estimate of the cost of the services consumed by that household.

Table 6.1 The Cheshire County Council study: net expenditure shares and service usage units

Sub-service heading	*Net expenditure %*	*Service usage unit*
Primary education	14.00	Number of pupils × cost
Education 11–15	20.00	Number of pupils × cost
Education 16 plus	12.10	Number of pupils × cost
Adult education	0.06	Number of students × cost
Special schools	2.90	Number of pupils × cost
Midday care	0.00	Pupils using
Free meals	2.30	Number of meals taken
Careers	0.30	Visits
Youth clubs	0.40	Pupils using
Home helps	1.20	Hours of visits
Meals on wheels	0.04	Number of meals
Aids	0.03	Number × type × cost
Adaptations	0.02	Number × type × cost
Other elderly soc. serv.	2.70	Users × type × cost
Physically handicapped	0.40	Users × type × cost
Mentally handicapped	0.90	Users × type × cost
Other children soc. serv.	1.80	Users × type × cost
Social workers	1.70	Visits × client type × cost
Public transport	1.70	Miles of bus travel
Roads	6.00	Car mileage
Museums	0.09	Visits
Country parks	0.20	Visits
Libraries	1.20	Books borrowed
Waste tips	0.50	Visits
All services studied	69.90	

How representative is Cheshire of the country as a whole? The first general point to make is that British local government in general is rather uniform in its provision of local public services, certainly compared with patterns in other countries. The reasons for this have to do with history, large size of units, legislation and standard-setting by central departments, and the dominance of professional groups in local authority decision-making (Stewart, 1983). This uniformity is probably more marked within the shire county authorities in terms of expenditure and population served. Cheshire can be said to be not untypical of such areas. For example, in the 'Shaw' classification of local authorities, as used by the Audit Commission, Cheshire is in one of the two commonest categories for shire counties, along with Avon, Essex, Gloucestershire, Hereford and Worcester, Kent and Warwickshire. Its levels of expenditure and grant-related expenditure per head are similar to averages for shire counties. Its demographic and socio-economic structure are similar to that of the nation as a whole. It has close to average values for a county on a number of indicators including population density, road mileage, children and 'additional educational needs' (Society of County Treasurers, 1986). In recent years it has been under both Conservative and Labour political control.

Where Cheshire and other shire counties probably do differ somewhat from a number of metropolitan and London local authorities is in the relative shares of spending devoted to broad service areas. It is generally fair to say that shire areas spend relatively more on roads, and in some cases on education, and less on social welfare services, than some of the more urban authorities. Since, as we shall see below, the distributional patterns for use of these different types of service is very different, the overall distributional pattern may differ systematically between shires and some urban areas. This suggests that parallel research in different kinds of areas would be a useful further step. But the overall significance of this point for the local government system as a whole should not be exaggerated; many metropolitan districts and outer London boroughs have social and political characteristics and spending levels not dissimilar to many shire counties.

The Cheshire study did not deal with a number of local services that are provided by the lower-tier district authorities. Currently the most important district service is council housing; however, the Government's recent housing legislation has had the effect of eliminating any charge on local taxation in respect of council housing, so that this service is no longer relevant to the issues discussed here. Relatively modest sums spent on other housing activities, private sector improvement and homelessness, will remain in the general expenditure accounts. Among the more important of the remainder are recreation, refuse collection, environmental health and planning. These district services account for quite a small share (about 14 per cent) of net expenditure by local authorities in shire areas. As with county services, we would judge that district services display varying distributional characteristics. Some, like environmental health and planning, are mainly public goods. Even so, there have been one or two studies which showed that services like street cleaning were more generous in affluent neighbourhoods (Webster, 1981, and Lineberry, 1977), and it would not be difficult to argue that the benefits of the greater amenity produced by planning are enjoyed most by the better off living on the edge of towns, in rural and conservation areas. There is a good deal of evidence on the participation profile of users of parks, sports centres and other recreational and leisure facilities (see Gratton and Taylor, 1985, and Veal, 1982), which shows a similar pattern in terms of income and class to that revealed for county leisure services below. Refuse collection may be argued to be more neutral in its distributional effects.

With these comments in mind, we would argue that the evidence from Cheshire County Council is not likely to be misleading for the local government system as a whole, at least in the majority of areas away from inner cities.

THE CHOICE OF COMPARISONS

In this section we discuss the kinds of comparisons which are most appropriate to make in the context of a paper concerned with the relationship between service distribution and local 'benefit' taxes. We start by considering the socio-economic dimension. In terms of what attributes of households do we wish to test for systematic variations in the use of services? This inevitably involves a consideration of the use of services by different types and sizes of households, so we discuss this first in order to identify a standardisation procedure to allow for it. We then discuss the specific dimensions chosen for comparison: income, socio-economic group and housing tenure. Having set up service usage comparisons across these groupings, we go on to consider the other side of the account, local tax liabilities. As well as discussing how to relate these comparisons to rates, the poll tax, and other options such as local income tax, we also discuss the treatment of rebates.

As soon as one considers the likely patterns of service usage one runs into the issue of household type and size. This is the dimension on which we would expect to find the greatest variation, for obvious reasons. Primary schools are used by households with children aged 5–11; meals on wheels are used by elderly one and two-person households; and so on. In other words, for some important services, a very uneven distribution between household types is inherent in the nature and purpose of the service; only certain groups are eligible or find the service relevant. These services could be described as deliberately redistributive, but primarily in the horizontal demographic sense, rather than the vertical socio-economic sense. We propose to discount these differences as not relevant to our analysis. In support of this position we would point out that the Government, in its Green Paper and subsequent legislation, also discounted this kind of horizontal redistribution. This is implicit in the notion that a uniform adult poll tax constitutes an approximation to a benefit tax.

In order to discount demographic effects it is desirable to adopt a standardisation procedure when making comparisons between socio-economic, income or tenure groups. This is because the demographic composition of different social and economic groups varies systematically; for example, there are more smaller households in the lower social and income groups. The procedure we adopted is to divide the sample households into nine groups: one-, two- and three-plus adult households; one adult with one and two-plus dependent children; two adults with one and two-plus dependent children; three-plus adults with one and two-plus dependent children. Usage rates were calculated for each demographic group within each social or economic group. These were then multiplied by the 'standardised' number of households in each demographic group within each social or economic group, where the standardised number was calculated on the assumption that the social or economic group had the same demographic structure as Cheshire as a whole. This procedure was equivalent to comparing usage rates within demographic groups across social/economic groups, but enabled us to build up an overall average picture for each social/economic group, taking account of all of the different demographic strata.

The first type of systematic comparison we wished to make is across the distribution of household income. Income is the best general measure of ability to pay, which represents the basic alternative principle of taxation to the benefit principle. In addition, economic theory suggests that for most goods and services, demand may be expected to rise with income, as we pointed out above when discussing Figure 6.1 and demand-based measures of benefit. A convenient and conventional way of comparing income groups is to divide the sample into five equal 'quintile' groups ranging from the lowest-income fifth to the highest. A simple way of expressing the degree and direction of inequality of a distribution of service usage (or taxes) is to calculate the ratio of the usage by the top quintile over the usage by the bottom quintile. A value near 1.0 indicates an even distribution; a value much less than one (down to zero) indicates a distribution in favour of the poor; a value much in excess of one (and up to infinity, in some cases) indicates a distribution in favour of the better off.

We also undertook the analysis using an equivalence scale to convert household incomes into 'equivalent incomes'. This is a method sometimes used, particularly in studies of income distribution, poverty and social security, to allow for the different incomes required by households of different size and structure to achieve a given standard of living. This can be argued to represent a truer measure of real income. Using equivalent incomes does not obviate the need to standardise for the effects of demographic structure on the usage of local services.

The second general type of comparison we made was in terms of socio-economic group (SEG for short), based on the occupation (or former occupation) of the head of household. The argument for this is partly the general one that SEG (or the similar concept of social class) is a better indicator of a household's long-term command over resources than the level of income in a particular year. More specifically, we would argue that for a number of social services SEG may actually be more closely associated with differences in access and preferences, and hence usage, than income. Middle-class people tend to be more articulate and better able to use services, especially those provided by middle-class professionals and bureaucrats. Certain types of services may also be used more as a matter of preference by middle-class people – libraries, museums and country parks. There is, for example, some evidence for this hypothesis in relation to health services (Le Grand, 1982).

The comparison was made in a similar way to that for income. The sample was divided into four broad SEG groupings: employers, managers and professionals; intermediate and junior non-manual; skilled manual; semi- and unskilled manual. Ratios of usage of the top to the bottom group were calculated and standardised as before. This time, the top and bottom groups were not identical in size, unlike the income quintiles, so allowance had to be made for the fact that the top group was 1.29 times the size of the bottom group.

The third type of comparison we made is between types of housing tenure. The reason for doing this was less clear-cut and we did not necessarily expect such distinctive distributional patterns. Part of any pattern observed will reflect the systematic differences in income and SEG between the tenures; for instance, we would generally expect owner-occupation to be associated with being better off. There is also a school of thought that there are systematic differences between tenures in patterns of consumption, preferences, voting, and social behaviour which are partly independent of social class. The main comparison we made is between standardised usage as between two tenure groups, owner-occupiers and tenants.

We place the main emphasis here on systematic distributions between broad social/economic groups, because these raise the most important issues of vertical equity as well as possible issues about incentives for migration. However, when considering the issue of benefit taxation there is also the question of variation between individuals, or individual households, in service usage. Local taxes may or may not show a general proportionality with benefits for broad groups, but they are less likely to do so at the level of individuals. This lack of match at individual level is perhaps as much of a problem for the theory behind benefit taxation as mismatch at group level. Certainly the Government's rhetoric in the Green Paper and elsewhere about the unfairness of rates would imply this. However, lack of space prevents an examination of this issue in this paper.

As far as local taxation options are concerned, we were obviously first and foremost interested in comparing the distribution of service usage (i.e. cost) as a whole with the distribution of the burden of the poll tax. Since we standardised service usage for demographic structure, we were obliged to standardise taxes in the same way. In practice this leads to a very simple answer with the poll tax. Standardisation meant we were comparing different social/economic groups as though they had the same demographic composition. But if they had the same demographic composition they would of course pay the same poll tax, before any rebates. Thus, the ratio of the total poll taxes paid by the best off and worst off groups would be simply the ratio of the size of the groups, whilst in per-household terms the ratio will be 1.0. It is also a consequence of the approach we were adopting of comparing shares of different groups that we did not need to worry about estimating the exact level of poll tax required to finance the same amount of services as were formerly financed by domestic rates.

It was of greatest interest, and perhaps sufficient for our general purpose, to show how service distributions compared with the poll tax. However, it was also of general interest, given the policy background, to make the comparison with the previous local domestic tax base, the rates. It was especially interesting to compare with rates because, as our earlier discussion showed, rates had been portrayed as a benefit tax, at least historically and in relation to certain classes of services. We were also in a good position to make the comparison, because the Cheshire survey contained data on actual rate payments. The questions attempted to elicit gross and rebated rents, and the gross figures were checked against the rating list.

Since the Layfield Committee (Department of the Environment, 1976) reported there has been growing recognition and support for the notion that the only sensible alternative or supplement to rates as a major local tax is a local income tax (see also Bennett, 1986, and Association of Metropolitan Authorities, 1986). The chief attempt to amend the 1988 Local Government Finance Bill – albeit an unsuccessful attempt – sought to band poll tax with respect to taxable income. Thus it would also be of interest to compare service distributions with the distribution of a possible local income tax. We did not attempt to do this in this paper, because there would have been technical problems in making accurate tax assessments for households in the sample, although we do comment briefly on the likely pattern. It could be argued that local income tax is not meant to be a benefit tax and therefore such a comparison is not meaningful in the same way as it would be with the other taxes. However, if our hypothesis that many services are used more by the better off is correct, the difference between benefit and ability to pay principles may be eroded. It would also be fair to say that local income tax ought to be compared with rebated rates or poll tax.

This leads us on to the last outstanding issue about the nature of the comparisons we made. Should we allow for rebates? Both rates and poll tax have rebate systems associated with them. Although similar in principle, the rebates associated with the poll tax are different in detail, particularly in that the unit shifts from the normal income unit (often the same as a household) to the individual. Also, the old rate rebate and supplementary benefit system, under which our Cheshire data were collected, allowed 100 per cent rebating, whereas the new system, introduced in April 1988, anticipated the local government finance reform by limiting rate/poll tax rebates to 80 per cent.

In the main analysis below we emphasise the comparison between service distributions and gross, unrebated tax liabilities. This is because we are concerned with the issue of benefit taxation. We would interpret the 'benefit tax' in its pure form to be the poll tax, or possibly the rates, without any rebate. Nobody pretends that the rebates have anything to do with the benefit principle. Rather, they are a limited concession to the ability-to-pay principle. Cynics might say that rebates are the necessary concession to enable the poll tax to be politically acceptable and collectable, or to enable objections to the basic inequity of the tax to be brushed aside.

However, we do attempt below to make further comparisons allowing for the rebates. Again, there are some technical difficulties here, for the reasons alluded to above. In general, we would expect rebates radically to reduce the tax contribution of the lowest income groups, but to make little difference in the middle of the range and none at the top. We would also expect that the rebate systems, given their basic similarity, would not have much differential effect on rates as against poll tax. There is a case, once rebates have been incorporated, for looking at the relationships between services and taxes for groups at the top of and in the middle of the economic spectrum, rather than those at the bottom.

THE EVIDENCE

Table 6.2 summarises the distributional pattern exhibited by each sub-service studied in Cheshire in relation to the four main dimensions of social/economic variation discussed above. The numbers in each cell of the table give the ratio of usage in the top income/social group to that in the bottom. Both crude and standardised ratios are shown, but for the reasons given above it is the standardised ratios which are of most interest. The ratios are very variable, ranging from zero (no usage in the top group) to infinity (no usage in the bottom group).

In trying to sum up this mass of data, we can say that there are four broad categories of case. First, we have services whose distribution is fairly even or neutral across the income or social spectrum in Cheshire. The largest services, primary and secondary (11–15) schooling, fall into this group, along with special schools and midday care. Education in the compulsory age groups has this characteristic because in Britain the use of private education is relatively small in scale (7 per cent nationally). The ratios for secondary education are inconsistent as between the two income measures, which is puzzling but might be related to private education. Public transport (bus use) also falls into this neutral category, which is rather more surprising.

Second, we have services which are clearly pro-poor or biased towards the less well off; these comprise free school meals, youth clubs, and a range of social services directed at the elderly and handicapped, including home helps, meals, aids and adaptations, day care and social work (although the latter is neutral in terms of SEG). This group of services is important and is targetted in a manner to effect a clear redistribution in favour of groups in need who tend to be poor. More detailed evidence on many of these services will be generated by the enhanced samples interviewed in later phases of the

Table 6.2 The Cheshire County Council study: usage ratios by income, socio-economic group and tenure group by sub-service (ratio of per-household usage by 'top' and 'bottom' groups with and without standardisation for household structure)

Sub-service heading	*Household income*		*Equivalent income*		*So.-Econ. group*		*Tenure Own vs. Rent*	
	Crude	*Stan.*	*Crude*	*Stan.*	*Crude*	*Stan.*	*Crude*	*Stan.*
Primary education	7.80	0.93	0.55	0.69	1.30	0.71	1.35	0.90
Education 11–15	25.50	7.20	0.53	0.51	0.96	0.76	1.47	0.97
Education 16 plus	inf	inf	inf	6inf	5.06	5.29	1.49	1.25
Adult education	4.50	14.30	2.42	5.41	1.45	0.50	1.35	0.99
Special schools	2.14	1.19	0.09	0.15	1.14	0.64	0.54	0.62
Midday care	8.40	1.08	0.58	0.44	1.33		1.39	0.62
Free meals	0.10	0.01	0.01	0.01	0.12	0.04	0.13	0.17
Careers	77.00	0.76	0.76	0.68	1.02	1.25	0.57	0.16
Youth clubs	0.00	0.00	0.00	0.00	0.00	0.00	1.41	0.18
Home helps	0.00	0.00	0.02	0.07	0.00	0.00	0.26	0.65
Meals on wheels	0.00	0.00	0.00	0.00	0.06	0.07	0.34	0.73
Aids	0.00	0.00	0.11	0.09	0.50	0.50	0.29	0.20
Adaptations	0.00	0.00	0.11	0.08	0.58	0.62	0.32	0.23
Other elderly soc. serv.	0.00	0.00	0.00	0.00	0.39	0.40	0.40	0.15
Physically handicapped	0.00	0.00	0.00	0.00	0.39	0.38	0.31	0.10
Mentally handicapped	0.08	0.60	0.08	0.08	0.00	0.00	0.02	0.01
Other children soc. serv.	0.70	2.10	0.56	0.41	1.19	0.88	2.14	0.42
Social workers	0.20	0.29	0.12	0.17	0.85	1.02	0.21	0.22
Public transport	2.30	1.60	1.21	0.99	0.70	0.89	0.87	0.43
Roads	10.60	4.24	6.23	5.02	2.66	2.26	2.81	1.50
Museums	1.40	1.40	0.82	0.64	1.30	0.75	1.62	1.51
Country parks	5.90	15.20	3.73	3.49	2.18	2.09	2.60	1.80
Libraries	2.00	0.93	1.50	1.46	2.22	1.85	1.56	0.93
Waste tips	2.50	1.80	0.82	2.30	1.92	1.84	2.23	1.24
All services studied	2.11	1.62	1.59	1.36	2.20	2.04	1.15	0.74

inf = infinity
stan. = standardised

Table 6.3 The Cheshire County Council study: distribution of the cost of all services used and of taxes by total household and equivalent income, socio-economic group and tenure (percentage)

	Services		*Rates*		*Poll tax*	
	Crude	*Stan.*	*Crude*	*Stan.*	*Crude*	*Stan.*
a Total household income						
Highest quintile	27.9	25.5	27.8	24.8	25.5	20.0
4th quintile	25.3	25.0	21.1	20.3	23.3	20.0
3rd quintile	14.9	16.2	18.1	17.9	21.0	20.0
2nd quintile	18.6	17.5	17.9	20.6	18.4	20.0
Lowest quintile	13.2	15.7	15.0	16.4	11.7	20.0
b Equivalent income						
Highest quintile	24.7	25.6	25.4	25.1	24.6	20.0
4th quintile	22.0	20.2	22.0	21.0	22.3	20.0
3rd quintile	20.0	20.2	19.6	19.5	20.9	20.0
2nd quintile	15.2	17.9	16.9	17.7	16.2	20.0
Lowest quintile	18.1	16.1	16.1	16.7	16.0	20.0
c Socio-economic group						
Professional etc.	33.0	32.0	40.0	35.1	26.7	26.0
Non-manual	25.0	26.5	20.0	21.3	18.7	20.0
Skilled manual	27.0	26.0	24.0	27.2	34.0	32.0
Semi/unskilled	15.0	15.7	16.0	16.4	20.6	20.0
d Tenure						
Owner-occupier	71.0	61.2	74.3	66.6	71.8	68.0
Rental	29.0	38.8	25.7	33.4	28.2	32.0

stan. = standardised

survey. However, the overall proportion of expenditure accounted for by these clearly redistributive services is not enormous (9.7 per cent).

Then we have a number of services which are clearly used much more by the better off. These include the well-known and important cases of 16-plus education and road use, but also several other services including country parks, waste tips and libraries (although libraries are more neutral on the criteria of total household income and tenure). We are not able to discuss at length the reasons for these patterns. The education case may be related to preferences, cultural expectations, attainment in earlier schooling, and income to support a longer period of full-time education in the general absence of maintenance grants for this group. The roads case (and some others like country parks and waste tips) relates to car ownership rates, and to factors like longer distance commuting associated with higher income. Taken together these services account for 20 per cent of expenditure. This fact immediately helps to show how it is that local services as a whole tend to favour the better off.

There are then a number of services where there is an apparent inconsistency between the results in terms of income and SEG, although the difference may reflect substantive behavioural factors. These services include adult education (pro-rich but oddly not pro-middle class), careers (pro-middle class but not pro-rich), museums and social services for children.

On the whole these results are consistent with our expectations, although there are some apparent surprises and inconsistencies. Some of these may be related to small sample numbers of users for some services. The results for housing tenure appear to be less clear-cut, with less tendency to favour the (admittedly very broad) owner-occupation group. More detailed analysis would be needed to tease out what the independent effects of tenure are, if any. There may be some tendency for council tenants to make more use of local authority services, for example because they have better information about them, but we have no direct evidence of this.

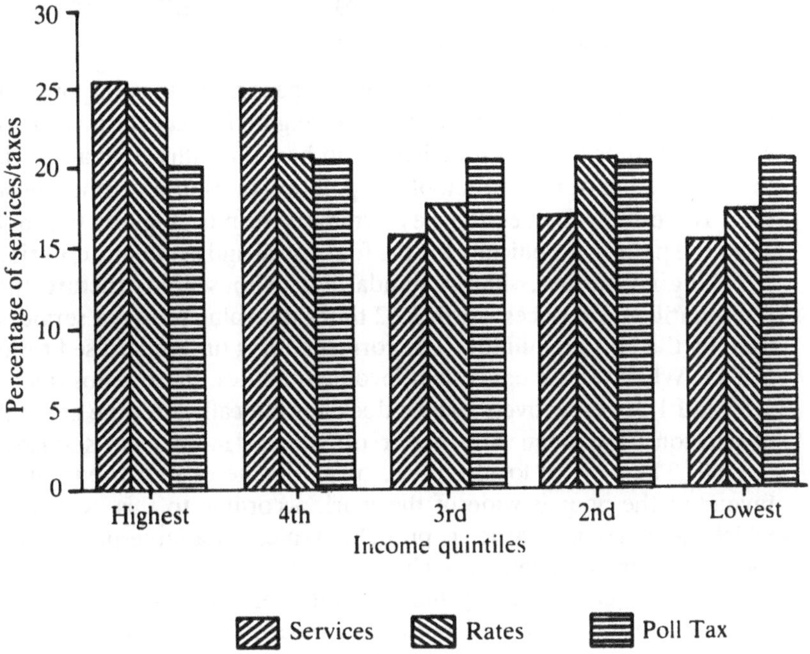

Figure 6.2 Distribution by total household income

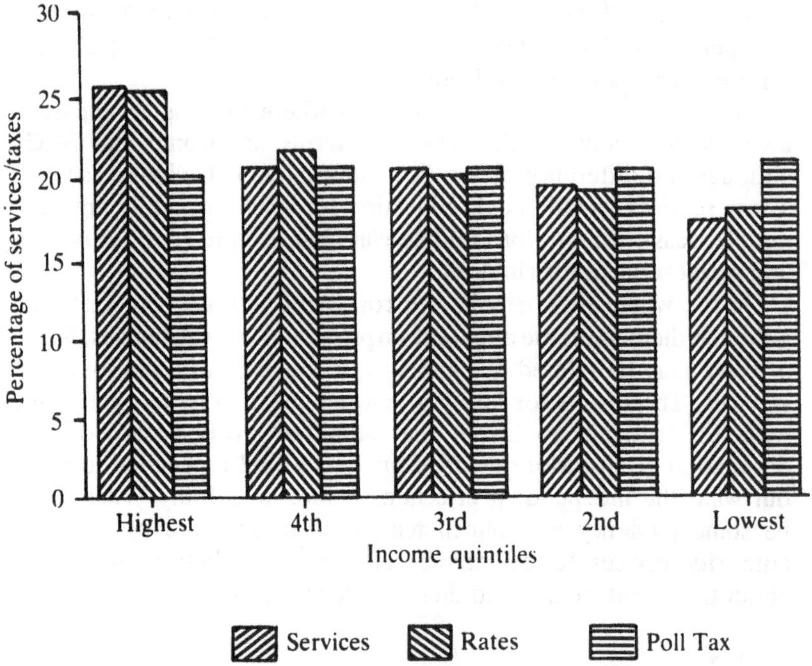

Figure 6.3 Distribution by equivalent income

We now come to the key issue in the paper. What is the overall distribution of service usage (valued, or weighted, in cost terms) when we add all these services together? And how does this compare with the distribution of the burden of the poll tax, rates or any other local tax? Table 6.3 provides the key summary results. Figures 6.2–6.5 show the pattern graphically for the four social and economic criteria.

Taking income first, when we standardise for household structure, the top quintile use services worth 1.62 times the value (cost) of services used by the bottom quintile. The corresponding unstandardised ratio is 2.11. When we use equivalent income quintiles, these ratios fall to 1.59 and 1.36 respectively, which does not radically alter the general conclusion. The financially better off do use more local services, overall. The view of local services as an engine of redistribution in favour of the poor is wide of the mark according to this evidence, which as we argued earlier is probably typical of a large part of the local government system as a whole.

We explained previously that the ratio of standardised poll tax liabilities between top and bottom income quintiles would be 1.0. Therefore we can say there is a systematic deviation from the benefit

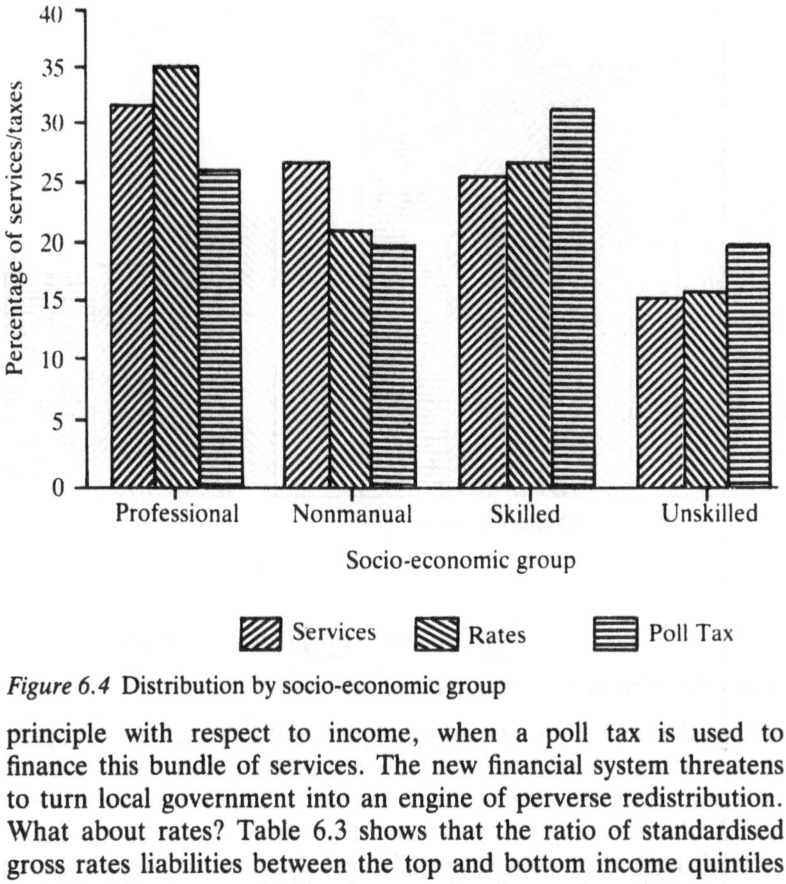

Figure 6.4 Distribution by socio-economic group

principle with respect to income, when a poll tax is used to finance this bundle of services. The new financial system threatens to turn local government into an engine of perverse redistribution. What about rates? Table 6.3 shows that the ratio of standardised gross rates liabilities between the top and bottom income quintiles is 1.51. This is remarkably close to the share of services that we have calculated. The closeness of it between services and rates is even more marked when we use equivalent incomes, and applies across all the income quintiles as is shown graphically in Figure 6.3.

When we turn to SEG, once we allow for the different size of the top and bottom groups, the results are rather similar. The service-use ratio (of professionals to semi/unskilled) is 2.04 (unstandardised 2.20). The standardised rates ratio is 2.14, again remarkably close to the usage ratio, whilst again standardised poll taxes would be equal. Figure 6.4 brings out another feature of the SEG distributions a little more clearly. The poll tax represents a systematic redistribution against manual and in favour of non-manual households, relative to both service distributions and rates.

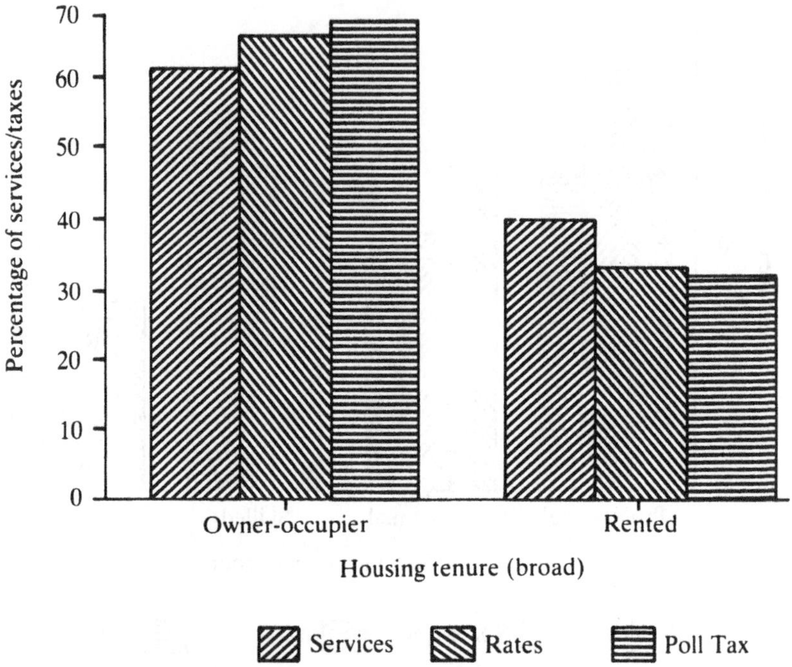

Figure 6.5 Distribution by housing tenure

The picture with housing tenure is slightly different. Owner-occupiers represent 68 per cent of households and therefore would pay 68 per cent of standardised poll tax, but their share of services when standardised is only 61.2 per cent. Even here, however, it can be argued that rates comes marginally closer to reflecting usage, with a share of 66.6 per cent.

So perhaps the dismissing of rates as a benefit tax by the Government and some of the economic theorists was a bit premature. Not only have we shown that the financially and socially better off tend to use more local services than the worse off, but we have also shown that the old rating system came quite close to matching these systematic differences. In this sense at least, rates appear to have been a reasonable benefit tax. By contrast, the poll tax is uniform in its incidence across these social and economic groups, and its underlying assumption of a uniformity of benefits is clearly false.

It was not possible to analyse in a similar way the incidence of a possible local income tax alternative. The difficulties and issues raised by the possibility were discussed earlier. It is clear, though, from crude data on the income levels associated with the income quintiles in Cheshire, that the distribution of such a tax would be different again from any of the distributions shown here, taking much more from the better off than rates and much more than the share of services consumed by the best off. So local income tax would almost certainly be redistributive in the way that the Government suggests. That, of course, would be its intention, since it is based on the principle of ability to pay. We should in any case compare it with rebated rates and poll tax. But what our results show is that the poll tax itself is also redistributive in a perverse manner.

CONCLUSIONS

The Government's case for introducing a poll tax appealed in substantial part to the benefit principal, which says people should pay for what they use of local services. There were other important arguments for the reform, to do with accountability, which are significantly flawed but beyond the scope of this paper. A plausible case can be made on grounds of equity and efficiency for a benefit tax at local level, although there are important qualifications to this theoretical case. But this case has so far been made without reference to any empirical evidence on the distribution of benefits, and the view that rates are no longer a proxy for benefits is pure assertion.

In this paper we draw evidence from a unique new survey carried out by a major and representative local authority. We discuss the methodological issues and propose a method of comparing the cost of services used between broad social and economic groups, whilst standardising for demographic effects.

The evidence on usage by service reveals dramatic variations between different services. Only about 10 per cent of expenditure goes on services which are clearly pro-poor in their distribution, mainly the personal social services. About 20 per cent of expenditure goes on services which are clearly biased in favour of the better off in their distribution, namely education over 16, roads, and some leisure services. The remainder of expenditure goes on services whose distribution is either relatively neutral or uniform, inconsistent as between different criteria, or not amenable to analysis by the same methodology owing to 'public good' characteristics.

Overall we can say that the better off use services costing 45–70 per cent more than those used by the least well off. This difference is quite closely matched by the old rating system, whereas the poll tax is of course distributed evenly across the social and economic spectrum.

Therefore we would argue that the Government was mistaken in its assertions: the poll tax loses any legitimacy it might have had as a benefit tax, and reversion to the rating system is a more attractive option if, indeed, a benefit tax is what is being sought.

This study has only begun to examine the issues which are opened up by the availability of service usage evidence. A number of such issues are immediately apparent and worthy of further study, either in the Cheshire context or elsewhere. First, there is the extent of individual household level variance in service usage and in tax liabilities, which is obviously also related to the benefit tax issue. Second, individual household level usage rates may be subject to statistical analysis to identify the relative importance of different determinants. Third, the enhanced sample data will enable a closer look to be given to some of the minority social services. Fourthly, and again benefiting from the fuller data, we could examine the influence of location, in the sense of type of area and accessibility to service points, on usage. Fifthly, a link could be made with important issues and evidence concerning attitudes to local services and expenditure, including the issue of external or non-user benefits. Finally, some international comparisons may be possible, insofar as comparable surveys have been undertaken by other countries.

REFERENCES

Association of Metropolitan Authorities (1986) *The AMA's Response to the Government's Green Paper 'Paying for Local Government'*, London: Association of Metropolitan Authorities.

Bennett, R.J. (1987) *A Local Income Tax in Britain: a Reappraisal of Theory and Practice*, London: Association of Metropolitan Authorities.

Bramley, G. (1987) 'Horizontal disparities and equalisation: a critique of "Paying for Local Government"', *Local Government Studies*, Jan/Feb 69–89.

Culyer, A. (1980) *The Political Economy of Social Policy*, Oxford: Martin Robertson.

Department of the Environment (1976) *Local Government Finance: Report of the Committee of Inquiry* (the Layfield Committee), Cmnd.6452, London: HMSO.

——(1986) *Paying for Local Government*, Cmnd.9714, London: HMSO.

Foster, C., Jackman, R. and Perlman, M. (1980) *Local Government Finance in a Unitary State*, London: Allen & Unwin.

Gratton, C. and Taylor, P. (1985) *Sport and Recreation: an Economic Analysis*, London: E. and F.N. Spon.

Hale, R., Hepworth, N. and Stonefrost, M. (1985) *Financing Local Government: a Different Approach*, London: Chartered Institute of Public Finance and Accountancy.

Head, J. (1974) *Public Goods and the Public Sector*, Durham, North Carolina: Duke University Press.

Jackman, R. (1986) 'Paying for Local Government', *Local Government Studies* 12:4.

King, D. (1984) *Fiscal Tiers: the Economics of Multi-level Government*, London: Allen & Unwin.

Le Grand, J. (1982) *The Strategy of Equality: Redistribution and the Social Services*, London: Allen & Unwin.

——(1987) 'Measuring the distributional impact of the welfare state: methodological issues', in R. Goodin and J. Le Grand *Not Only the Poor: the Middle Classes and the Welfare State*, London: Allen & Unwin.

Lineberry, R. (1977) *Equality and Urban Policy: the Distribution of Municipal Public Services*, Beverley Hills: Sage.

Musgrave, R. and Musgrave, P. (1980) *Public Finance in Theory and Practice*, New York: McGraw-Hill.

Smith, S. (1988) 'Should UK local government be financed by a poll tax?', *Fiscal Studies* 9:1.

Society of County Treasurers (1986) *Block Grant Indicators 1986–7*, London: Society of County Treasurers.

Stewart, J. (1983) *Local Government: the Condition of Local Choice*, London: Allen & Unwin.

Stigler, G. (1957) 'The tenable range of functions of local government', in Joint Economic Committee *Federal Expenditure Policy for Economic Growth and Stability*, Washington DC.

Tiebout, C. (1956) 'A pure theory of local expenditure', *Journal of Political Economy* 64:5.

Veal, A. (1982) *Recreation in 1980: Participation Patterns in England and Wales*, Report to the Sports Council and the Countryside Commission, London: North London Polytechnic.

Webster, B. 1981, 'The distributional effects of local government services: a framework for analysis', in S. Leach and J. Stewart (eds) *Approaches in Public Policy*, London: Allen & Unwin.

7 Reform of local taxation in Germany

Criteria and proposals

Horst Zimmermann

Editor's Note: This paper was revised in October 1989, before German unification took place, and it refers throughout to West Germany. Despite the subsequent unification, the issues which are discussed in the paper still remain on the political agenda.

INTRODUCTION

This paper looks at local government finance from a West German perspective, considering in turn the criteria for good local taxes; the achievements and deficiencies of the 1969 local tax reforms; and some proposals for reforms to local business taxes. It finishes with some concluding remarks.

It is hoped that all of this will be of interest to researchers in other countries who are looking at comparable issues. But perhaps of chief interest to them will be the discussion of the criteria for good local taxes – as these criteria have been developed in Germany – and the discussion of the difficulties of designing local business taxes.

Before proceeding, it is helpful to make a few remarks about the German federal system. The Federal Republic of Germany incoporates an intermediate state level of government between the federal government and local authorities. This state level consists of ten area states, two city states, and Berlin with a special status. At the local level are 8,506 communities and 328 counties (of which 91 are city-counties, where the city and county are coterminous).

The functions to be fulfilled at the local level are not clearly defined in the German constitution, because the states were given the responsibility of delegating powers to their local governments. Article 28 guarantees in broad terms only the existence of communities, and entitles them to manage 'all affairs of the local community that are their own responsibility within existing laws', but it does not itself assign specific well-defined functions. Though local authorities depend, therefore, on the individual state for their powers, there is considerable similarity among the states as to the division of functions between state and local government (Zimmermann, 1981). The main functions at the local level are social policies, which account for 23 per cent of expenditure, school buildings and their maintenance, which account for 10 per cent, and health, sports and recreation, which account for 9 per cent.

As far as local revenues are concerned, 35 per cent come from tax revenue, 23 per cent from fees and charges, and 27 per cent from grants from upper-level governments (Karrenberg and Münstermann, 1988, figures for 1985). Local taxes as part of local revenue are guaranteed better by the constitution than local functions. Article 106 rules that communities shall receive a share of the income tax revenue and are entitled to taxes on real property and business as well as to local excise taxes. So any changes in the system of local taxation can occur only with due respect to rather precise constitutional provisions, and – with the exception of the small local excise taxes – must occur through federal legislation. It is possibly under this strong national influence that a coherent set of criteria has been developed over time as to what functions a local tax should fulfil.

CRITERIA FOR LOCAL TAXES

To evaluate either an existing local tax system or proposals for reform, a list of criteria for a 'good' local tax is needed. The following criteria are mostly those suggested by Zimmermann and Postlep (1980). Some of these criteria will be accepted by most scholars in the field. Others may be specific to the German situation but may still provide a stimulus to further thought.

The criteria are grouped into three categories, the first being related to a national perspective while the second and third are related to the special features of local government (Zimmermann, 1987a, p. 44–51). Between these two views, national and local, the emphasis can vary. On the one hand, it is argued that a consistent system of taxation in the nation as a whole has to prevail, and that the needs of local authorities must be fitted round this, even if the resulting local tax system shows some deficiencies. On the other hand, there is a widespread feeling that local government has lost much of its original importance over the last decade, and should now be strengthened. Therefore the need for a good local tax system should be emphasised and at least some trade-off with the consistency of the national tax system should be accepted, though not to an unlimited degree. In any case, the criteria for good local taxes need be applied only to the total bundle of local taxes and need not apply fully to each individual tax.

As far as the national perspective is concerned, a local tax should be judged under the same criteria as any federal or state tax. It should not contradict national social policy objectives or national economic objectives concerning resource allocation, distribution and stabilisation. If aimed at individuals, it should follow ability-to-pay principles, and it should be inexpensive to collect, for both the Government and the taxpayer. A special criterion is important for the reform of local business taxes to be discussed below: this is the ability of a tax to be handled by the country-of-destination-principle at the border, as happens with value added tax and national excise taxes. Should the country-of-origin principle be introduced in the European Community after 1992, then this criterion may be of less importance.

The national perspective criteria, though they are always important, need not be applied with equal rigour to each local tax. This was acknowledged, though rather late, after the abolition in 1979 of the local payroll tax (which was part of the local business tax). As a tax on business that was not related to profits, the payroll tax constituted a specific burden on business if no profits were made, and this seemed undesirable under national economic policy objectives. As a local tax, however, the payroll tax had some merit, as shown in some later proposals which included this tax – though often only implicitly.

The other two groups of criteria, which are related to the special features of local government, are outlined in Table 7.1. All these criteria are usually included in German discussions, but only two will be looked at more closely here, because they will be important for the discussion of current reform proposals:

a A very important criterion, especially from the viewpoint of fiscal federalism, is what the Advisory Council of the Federal Ministry of Finance has termed the 'balance of interests' (Wissenschaftlicher Beirat, 1982). It implies that there are two groups in a community which both receive local services and which should therefore be subject to local taxation: these groups are private households, and business. So a system of local taxation should contain a large tax on private households and, if possible, a similarly large tax on local business. Such a system should help to establish links between city governments and both of these groups. It should help to make city treasurers interested in households and businesses, because they know that their tax money is coming from these two groups. It is more difficult to make taxpayers aware of a clear link between themselves and local government. For this purpose, local taxes should be perceptible to local taxpayers, and if possible local authorities should be allowed to set their own rates. It must be admitted that it is hard to measure the benefits from local services to individual households and businesses: where this can be done it seems to suggest that charges rather than taxes might be the appropriate source of finance.

b Local tax rate setting should be allowed for reasons other than the one just noted. Whether local tax rate setting has to be applied to all local taxes or to only one or two major ones, is a matter to be decided politically.

One further point needs to be made here. This is that local taxes on business should have – or at least include – a tax base other than profits. This will help to ensure that local tax revenues do not fluctuate too much over periods of boom and recession. To achieve this it has first to be decided nationally what level of local (non-profit) business taxes is acceptable, and then incorporate this level in local rather than state or federal taxes.

Table 7.1 Specific criteria for local taxes

Pertaining to vertical relations (local vis-à-vis *upper levels)*
1 Small revenue fluctuations during business cycles
2 Revenue growth proportionate to local economic growth
3 Derivation of tax revenue from local tax base
4 Making taxes perceptible; balance of interests
5 Protection against one-sided local economic structure
Pertaining to horizontal relations (between local governments)
1. Distribution of tax potential according to local expenditure needs
2. Flexibility of local tax rates.

Source: Zimmermann and Postlep (1980) p.248 (supplemented)

ACHIEVEMENTS AND DEFICIENCIES OF THE 1969 LOCAL TAX REFORM

In 1968, the year before the reform laws were passed, local authorities derived 32 per cent of their total revenue from taxes (Seiler, 1981, p.516). Among their taxes, the business tax (*Gewerbesteuer*) clearly dominated, with 78 per cent of all tax revenue, followed by the property tax (*Grundsteuer*), with 17 per cent. The other smaller taxes amounted to less than 6 per cent between them. The largest part of the business tax revenue was derived from business profits, followed by smaller amounts from business capital and payrolls. This local tax system had evolved immediately after the Second World War, whereas before and after the First World War the largest local tax had been a kind of local income tax, followed by the property tax and supplemented by a rather small business tax (Seiler, 1981, p.516).

The situation before 1969 was deemed untenable. Private households were fiscally connected with their communities only through the rather small property tax and the few excise taxes. The business tax relied heavily on profits which meant that, at any point in time, there were very large differences between economically well-off communities and others; it also meant that, over time, the business tax revenue varied tremendously with boom and recession, owing to the high elasticity of profits with respect to GNP.

As far as communities were concerned, the main merit of the fiscal reform of 1969 consisted in reducing the dependency of local budgets on the business tax. At the same time, the communities were included in income tax sharing. A certain percentage of the income tax collected within a state is set aside for communities. In 1988 the percentage was 15 per cent. The amount distributed to each community does not depend precisely on its share of the tax base: rather it depends on what its share would be if all single people with incomes over DM 32,000 and all couples with incomes over DM 64,000 were deemed to have incomes of DM 32,000 and DM 64,000. This 'cap' on the income to be included reduces the spread between rich and poor communities and prevents city treasurers from being keen to attract millionaires as inhabitants. Unfortunately, communities are not allowed to set the tax rate for their share. Therefore the link works only one way. City treasurers knows where their money comes from, but citizens usually do not know that they contribute income tax to their communities; still less do they have any idea of how much they contribute. The laws of 1969 introduced into the constitution a provision that local authorities could be granted the power to set their own income tax rates, but so far this has not been done. Interestingly, though, this power does appear in some recent proposals.

The replacement of part of the business tax revenue by the income tax share had several effects. First of all, it re-established the 'balance of interests', which had been tipped towards business since the time of the Second World War. Secondly, total local tax revenue fluctuates much less during the course of cycles than it did before. Thirdly, the volume of local tax revenue has increased more since 1969 than it would have done with the old business tax; for the business tax was so overstretched under the pre-1969 regime that it would have been hard to increase local tax revenue through that channel alone. The 1969 reforms did not solve all the problems of local taxation. To start with the business tax, its inherent weaknesses were not touched in the reform of 1969 – only its weight in the system was reduced. The professions, which before the Second World War had been subject to the business tax, were still exempt. The public sector was not covered at all, and the fluctuation with business cycles was still rather strong, because the business profits part of this tax still dominated.

The property tax did not change in the reform at all. It is grossly underdeveloped in the German local tax system. To a major degree this is due to an outdated assessment, which last took place in 1964. However, even if a recent assessment had been made, the danger is that local governments would hesitate to use this instrument strongly, because for the first time since between the wars this would face them with the need to stand up in front of their whole electorates and argue for higher taxes. German communities are no longer used to doing this.

In 1979 the payroll tax part of the business tax was abolished. This occurred exclusively under national economic policy objectives, and the fact that it had been a rather useful local tax was not taken up in the discussion. Its abolition left large revenue gaps, particularly in those cities which relied on subsidised industries with little or no profits – mainly the Ruhr cities – so that compensation payments had to be made for quite some time. Instead of abolishing the payroll tax, it would have been better to have made it a mandatory part of the business tax. The payroll part had been optional and was used in some states only. The idea of a compulsory payroll element in the local business tax can be found in some recent proposals. Quite apart from the removal of the payroll tax part of the local business tax, the base of the business tax was reduced several times after 1969, and tax exemptions were strongly extended, so that today less than one-third of all businesses to which the tax applies actually pay this tax.

Taking together the deficiencies of the reform of 1969 and the influence of changes since then, the situation is broadly as follows:

a The income tax share as a link to private households seems acceptable, but it should be supplemented by the power for tax rates to be set locally.
b The property tax is underdeveloped. Foreign experience suggests that a significant local property tax is a very useful local tax, as long as it is not too high.
c The business tax is not acceptable in its present form. Even under national policy objectives such a fragmentary tax is not tenable, and there are further problems at the local level in view of the small number of taxpayers.

It is a widely-held opinion that another local tax reform has to be made because of the weaknesses of the present business tax. This explains why new proposals are made continuously about how to change this important and – due to its different tasks – difficult tax. The following discussion is restricted to proposals concerning reform of the business tax (see also Zimmermann, 1988); other proposals (for instance Haller, 1987) are left out of consideration because they would abolish the business tax. Because there are so many proposals available, it is important to remember the criteria for a 'good' local tax which were discussed earlier.

REFORM PROPOSALS FOR THE LOCAL BUSINESS TAX

When the principles of local taxes are discussed in the theory of fiscal federalism it is usually assumed – implicitly or explicitly – that local taxes are levied on private households, not on businesses. This would be adequate in a world with short commuting distances, where people lived and worked in the same small local authority area. Commuting distances are now large, however, and giant communities would be needed if people were to be considered as living and working in the same area. So, today, dominantly business areas and dominantly residential areas exist side by side, even in small conglomerations. To keep each type of area interested in its dominant type of taxpayer, and to keep the authorities in mixed communities interested in both businesses and households, the 'balance of interest' has to be guaranteed, and this makes it necessary for the local tax mix to include a business tax (see Schmidt, Schoser and Zimmermann in Bennett and Zimmermann, 1986).

Whereas it is rather easy to establish a local tax on people (be it a separate local tax like a property tax or a shared tax like the German income tax), it is much more difficult to establish a local business tax. The main problem seems to stem from multi-unit firms with subsidiaries in several communities, for this means that the tax base of each such firm has to be broken down between the different communities. This is quite easy to do with a local property tax, because parcels of property are usually clearly defined. However, if items such as business profits, assets or value added are chosen as the tax base, then the breakdown becomes much more difficult. This becomes quite clear when the different proposals for a German local business tax are considered.

The tax base of the present business tax makes use of the calculations of business profits and business capital that are already calculated for other taxes. Only a few additions and subtractions have to be made, and these are quite easy to handle. Therefore the compliance cost of this tax is not high, and this constitutes one of its advantages. Starting from this, and bearing in mind that the deficiencies of the business tax are mainly due to the fragmentary tax base and to taxpayer definitions, it is easy to imagine modifications to this tax which would make it an acceptable tax on business.

For that purpose, one could reintroduce the payroll part of the tax by making it compulsory for all communities. This payroll part could be introduced into the present business tax as a separate factor, and then communities could be allowed to levy one tax rate on all components together. Moreover, one could easily include additional taxpayers like the professions, and this, together with a reduction in exemptions, should make it possible to reduce the tax rate considerably (Zimmermann, 1987b). All of this would fit the general tax reform tendency – noticeable both nationally and internationally – of simultaneously widening tax bases and lowering tax rates.

For quite some time it seemed that proposals such as these had no chance of being discussed: the business tax as such was pronounced dead. However, the fact that a recent proposal again uses the term '*Gewerbesteuer*' means that a modification of this tax no longer seems as improbable as it did a few years ago.

As an alternative idea, however, several proposals exist to introduce a local value added tax. They have in common the idea – expressed either explicity or implicitly – that local value added should be the basis of a new tax. The present *Umsatzsteuer* had for some years the legal second name of *Mehrwertsteuer*, which is synonymous with value added. This national tax approximates to value added by deducting the tax on purchased goods and services from the tax bill for goods and services sold. The proposals for a local tax, though, envisage a true value added tax, which means that the technique would be totally different. Also, it should be noted that any local value added tax does not aim at local consumption, but only at the local share of value added of any good being produced, processed or sold in the community. Such a tax may be contrasted with a tax on local consumption, like a local sales tax – whether on sales in general or on specific goods like beverages. A sales tax automatically taxes value added in total, and ignores the fact that some of this value added has usually been produced elsewhere.

The best known proposal for a local value added tax was made in 1982 by the Advisory Council of the Federal Ministry of Finance (see Schmidt, 1987, for a detailed description, and see Arbeitsgruppe Steuerreform, 1987, for a modified proposal). The tax base for each firm would be the sum of its payroll, profits, interest paid, and rent. It would have to be paid by businesses and the professions, and also by government institutions, which would be important, for instance, in small university towns. When federal or state institutions provide jobs in a community, the local authority services provided for these jobs are often the same as those provided for jobs in the private sector, and thus they should be compensated for. The argument that this would result only in transfers from one public pocket to another overlooks the different interests of different levels of government.

A second and widely-discussed proposal for a value added tax was made by the association of German cities (*Deutscher Städtetag*), representing mainly the larger communities (*Deutscher Städtetag*, 1986). It used the term *Gewerbesteuer* and proposed its 'revitalization'. Looking at it closely, it appears as another form of a value added tax, because the proposed tax base consists of profits, rent, interest paid, and payroll. An interesting feature is the possibility of weighting the various elements differently so that under national economic policy perspectives the elements other than profits could be weighted lower in order to reach a compromise between the objectives of a local tax and of national taxation. Taxpayers are to include the professions and some other currently excluded taxpayers, but not government institutions.

Any local value added tax would have the advantage of allowing for locally-set tax rates. The tax base could be very broad, so that the tax rates could be low. This would certainly mean that the tax base would have to include payrolls, and this makes it the more difficult to understand why this element of the existing business tax was abolished in 1979. A disadvantage of these proposals is to be seen in the need for an effectively new tax base, whereas the present business tax builds on elements which are already necessary for other taxes. Also, the spread in value added tax revenues between communities seems to be just as wide as that of the business tax, so that the need for fiscal equalisation between communities would not be reduced.

If it is thought that there should be value added taxation at the local level, and if, as in Germany, there is a national value added tax, then an apparently elegant idea would be to include local authorities in the tax-sharing scheme which already exists between federal and state levels. This would mean that the tax base of value added taxes at each level would be the same, tax administration could occur simultaneously and would be much cheaper, and additional compliance costs would be nil.

The main problem is that it seems practically impossible to allow for locally-set tax rates for the local share of a shared tax (see Rau and Rieger, 1981). This may seem strange, considering that some proposals do contain such a share and distribute it to local budgets on the basis of a specially-calculated local tax base. However, there is a great difference in the legal prerequisites. A transfer of funds from a centrally-collected amount of value added tax to a local budget means a transfer within the public sector, and can easily be managed by means of indicators, if they represent the regional tax base sufficiently well. However, a separate tax law would be needed if local tax rate setting was allowed. Such a tax law would be needed to cover compulsory transfers from the private sector to the public sector and, according to the standards of tax legislation, has to be specified very precisely. One problem, which still seems to be unresolved, is how the local tax bill should be calculated for the local subsidiary of an out-of-town company.

For these reasons, another proposal provides a local share in the value added tax, but without a locally-set tax rate; instead, this proposal retains a sharply reduced business tax with a locally-set tax rate (see Füst and Willemsen, 1986). However, the base of the locally set tax – and hence its feasible yield – would be very small, so this proposal is not very promising.

Thus there is a dilemma. On the one hand there is an elegant solution, using tax-sharing of the value added tax; on the other hand there is the desire to keep a reasonable yield for locally-set taxes. One solution to this dilemma, as made in several recent proposals, is to include communities in the tax-sharing of the value added tax and at the same time activate the possibility of having locally-set tax rates on the income tax share. (These proposals are contained in Albers, 1987, where the share of the value added tax is meant for the counties instead of the communities, Bangemann, 1988, and

Arbeitsgemeinschaft selbständiger Unternehmer, 1988.)

Such proposals would undoubtedly lead to a major reform of the local tax system, because both the large local taxes would have to be changed in an interrelated way. The result would be a continuing 'balance of interests' between private households and businesses on one hand and the community on the other. The power for local authorities to set some tax rates would be preserved in the local tax system as such, where one would expect it in the first place, namely in relation to local taxes on private households. If the power for local authorities to set their own tax rates on the income tax share was introduced, then citizens would know for the first time in decades what they themselves contribute to local tax revenues (at least this is so if the small property tax and the other small local taxes are left out of the picture for the moment). Incidentally, the fact that so many proposals have been made to introduce locally-set tax rates on the income tax share suggests that technical problems, which until recently were usually given as the reasons for not having it, apparently cannot be as serious as were previously thought. However, much remains to be clarified; in particular the formula by which the value added tax share is to be distributed to communities has to be developed, but like any allocation within the public sector, this problem should be tolerably easy to solve.

There is, though, another proposal for reforming the local taxation of businesses. This proposal is wider-reaching than the proposals of discussed so far, so it needs to be discussed separately (see Kronberger Kreis, 1988).

Instead of the business tax, a different tax (*Betriebsteuer*) is proposed for value added; but in contrast to the national value added tax, the base for this tax is to be derived by subtracting the input value of goods and services purchased from the output value of goods and services which are sold (instead of subtracting amounts of tax). It is proposed to take 1.5 per cent of this value added as the tax base, and taxpayers are to include businesses and the professions. The exemption of federal and state government units is to be offset by the introduction of a special grant. Such a grant is a new element in the discussion. As far as the communities are concerned, this new grant would possibly be a sufficient compensation for the local services provided for the exempt establishments.

Instead of the income tax share, an 'inhabitant's tax' (*Einwohnersteuer*) is proposed, with the local tax base being set as 10 per cent of the income tax base. This would abolish the 'cap', but the cap could probably be inserted easily in this proposal if this was desired for political reasons. Finally, the present property tax is also included in the system, though its size has not been specified.

The new element in this proposal is the fact that all of the three local tax bases described so far are to be part of a wide local tax base, and the locally-set tax rates would apply to this cumulative tax base. The basic technique of fitting several such components into one tax is already present in the existing business tax. The federal law defines the separate tax bases, multiplies them with separate factors, and then adds the results to produce a local tax base. Communities are then allowed to apply their own locally-set tax rates to this federally-predetermined tax base.

By allowing a local tax rate on the new threefold tax base, this proposal contain the highest degree of local fiscal autonomy, at least inasmuch as this is expressed in the power to set tax rates. It would mean a very broad tax, and communities would not be able to tax business more than private households, or vice versa, but only simultaneously in a relation which would be fixed in the federal law. The 'balance of interests' would be realised through the relation of different tax base elements. This proposal would certainly entail the broadest local tax reform, but some components, like the property tax, should be easy to handle.

CONCLUDING REMARKS

The starting point for another local tax reform, if it should occur, would certainly be the erosion of the business tax, which in the medium term makes it necessary to act. The reform could be small, if the present business tax was modified or if a local value added tax was introduced, because then the right for local authorities to set tax rates would remain untouched and the local income tax share would not have to be changed. However, a major reform would be necessary if local governments were to be included in the value added tax sharing scheme, or if the final proposal discussed was adopted.

Each of the three possibilities seems to be acceptable in principle, because each contains solutions which correspond to the more important criteria of a 'good' local tax. It is impossible to say at the moment which of the possibilities is the best. But one can assume that a major reform will be necessary in at least ten to fifteen years, if nothing is done now, because of the large and growing problems of the business tax. And it would be best not to have major reforms both now and also in ten to fifteen years' time.

REFERENCES

Albers, W. (1987), 'The reform of local business taxes in Germany', *Environment and Planning C: Government and Policy* 5:1.
Arbeitsgemeinschaft Selbständiger Unternehmer (1988) 'Das Fossil muss weg!', *Unternehmer* 4, pp. 18–19.
Arbeitsgruppe Steuerreform (1987) *Steuern der Neunziger Jahre*, Stuttgart.
Bangemann, M. (1988), 'Geschickter Vorstoss', *Wirtschaftswoche* 42.
Bennett, R.J. and Zimmermann, H. (eds) (1986) *Local Business Taxes in Britain and Germany*, London: Anglo-German Foundation.
Deutscher Städtetag (1986) 'Vorschlag des Deutschen Städtetages zur Umgestaltung der Gewerbesteuer', *Der Städtetag* 39.
Füst, W. and Willemsen, A. (1986) *Alte Steuer - Gute Steuer?*, Cologne.
Haller, H. (1987) *Zur Frage der Zweckmässigen gestalt Gemeindlicher Steuern*, Frankfurt.
Karrenberg, H. and Münstermann, E. (1988) 'Gemeindefinanzbericht 1988,' *Der Städtetag* 41.
Kronberger Kreis (1988) *Die Reform des Gemeindesteuersystems*, Argumente zur Wirtschaftspolitik, No.17, Frankfurt: Frankfurter Institut.
Rau, G. and Rieger, G. (1981) *Möglichkeiten einer Gemeindebeteiligung an der Umsatzsteuer*, St Augustin: Insitut fur Kommunalwissenschaften.
Schmidt, K. (1987) 'The case for a local net value-added tax for municipalities', *Government and Policy* 5:1.
Seiler, G. (1981) 'Gemeinden III: Finanzen' *Handwörterbuch der Wirtschaftswissenschaft, Vol.3*, Stuttgart.
Wissenschaftlicher Beirat beim Bundesministerium der Finanzen (1982) *Gutachten zur Reform der Gemeindesteuern in der Bundesrepublik Deutschland*, Bonn.
Zimmermann, H. (1981) *Studies in Comparative Federalism: West Germany*, Washington DC: Advisory Commission on Intergovernmental Relations.
——(1987a) 'British and German local business taxes under criteria for a "good" local tax', *Government and Policy* 5:1.
——(1987b) 'Reform des kommunalen Steuersystems', *Dezentralisierung des Politischen Handelns*, Melle: Institut fuer Kommunalwissenschaften.
——(1988) 'Fortsetzung der Gemeindesteuerreform?', *Der Gemeindehaushalt*, 89.
Zimmermann, H. and Postlep, R.-D. (1980) 'Beurteilungsmaßstäbe für Gemeindesteuern', *Wirtschaftsdienst* 60.

8 Property taxation in France

Remy Prud'homme and Françoise Navarre

INTRODUCTION

In France, as in a number of other countries, there are many forms of property taxes and several levels of government to raise them. There are four levels of government in France: the central government; the twenty-two regions that have had the status of local authorities from 1983; the counties (*départements*), of which there are about one hundred; and the communes, which are very diverse in size and in population, and very numerous – there are about 36,000. The three subnational tiers of government have a degree of fiscal autonomy in the sense that they can decide, within certain limits, the rates of the various taxes which are ascribed to them, even though they cannot create taxes.

Table 8.1 indicates the different types of property tax allocated to the various levels of government. The main property taxes raised at the subnational level are the land taxes, the business tax, and the vehicle taxes. The land taxes consist of two taxes: a tax on non-developed land (*impôt foncier non-bâti*, IFNB), based mostly on agricultural land; and a tax on developed land (*impôt foncier bâti*, IFB) based on residential, commercial and industrial buildings. Both taxes are assessed on the rental value of properties. The business tax (*taxe professionnelle*), levied on enterprises, is only in part a property tax. The tax base is mixed and includes the value of the assets of the enterprise and a fraction of the wages paid by the enterprise. It is meant to be a tax on business profits or activities, for which this strange tax base is a crude proxy.

This discussion of local property taxes will focus on the two communal land taxes. The regional vehicle purchase tax is too specific to be very interesting, and has a low yield anyway. The same can be said of the counties' vehicle ownership tax. The counties' and regions' land taxes

Table 8.1 Main property taxes by type of tax and level of government, 1988

Tax type	*Central government*	*Regions*	*Counties (Départements)*	*Communes*
Property ownership	Wealth tax[1]	Vehicle tax Land taxes[3] Business tax[4]	Land taxes[3] Business tax[4]	Land taxes[3] Business tax[4]
Property sales	Property sales tax[2]	Vehicle purchase tax[5] Surcharge on property sales tax	Land sales tax[6]	
Property transmission	Inheritance tax			

Notes:

1 A 'tax on large fortunes' (*Impôt sur les Grandes Fortunes*) was introduced in 1981, repealed in 1986, and then re-established in 1988 under the name of *Impôt de Solidarité sur la Fortune*.

2 *Droits de mutations et d'enregistrement.*

3 *Impôt Foncier non-bâti* and *Impôt Foncier bâti.*

4 *Taxe professionnelle*

5 *Impôt sur les cartes grises*

6 *Taxe sur la publicité foncière*

are similar to the communal land taxes. Indeed, each piece of property is taxed three times: first by the commune in which it is located, at the rate decided by the commune, second by the county in which it is located, at the rate decided by the county, and third, by the region in which it is located: the analysis that will be developed for communes could be developed for counties and for regions, but would probably not add much. The exclusion of the business tax is justified by the mixed characteristics of the tax, which is usually not considered as a property tax.

Much of the analysis will be based on a sample of 200 communes in the Ile de France region. This region was chosen because the data, and particularly the data on income by commune (which is usually hard to obtain in France) was available. But there are reasons to expect Ile de France to be representative of France for our purposes. It is the largest county. It includes about 1,300 communes, which are very diverse in terms of factors such as size, income and political persuasion, and it can be considered as representative of the country. Our sample of 200 communes was drawn randomly from the population of 1,300 communes, with probabilities increasing with respect to size, in order to have a sufficient number of large communes.

The paper is organised as follows. First we try to show the practical importance of the local land taxes in relation to property values and to other taxes. The next section is devoted to one of the most important characteristics of local land taxes (and of local taxes in general): the disparities that exist in tax bases between local governments. We then study the behaviour of local governments, in terms of rate setting, in the face of existing disparities. Finally there is a concluding section.

THE IMPORTANCE OF LOCAL PROPERTY TAXATION

The importance of local land taxes in France can be related to local taxation, to property taxation in general, to total taxes in France, and to the market value of the property taxed. The first three measures, are shown in Table 8.2. This table shows quite clearly that local land taxes represent the bulk of property taxation in France, accounting for nearly 89 per cent of all property taxes raised by all levels of government. In other words, property taxation is predominantly a local government function.

Table 8.2 Relative importance of local land taxation in France, 1986

	Tax on non-developed land	*Tax on developed land*	*Total local land taxes*
As % of:			
local taxes	4.9	22.5	27.4
property taxes	15.8	72.9	88.7
total taxes in France	0.3	1.6	1.9

Sources: OECD, *Conseil National des Impôts*, 1987; *Ministère de L'Intérieur*, 1988

Secondly, land taxation accounts for about 27 per cent of local government taxation. This is by no means negligible, but is much less than the levels in countries like the United Kingdom or the United States. The most important local tax in France is the business tax, which accounts for about half local government tax income. There is also a housing tax that represents about 20 per cent of local tax income. These two taxes have some land property tax features, but are not generally considered as such. The ratio of land taxes to local government revenues is not the same for each level of government. The figure given above, 27 per cent, refers to all levels taken together. For communes, the most important level of government, and the one for which the analysis will be conducted, this figure is about 28 per cent.

Thirdly, Table 8.2 shows that land taxation – and more generally property taxation – is relatively unimportant in the overall French tax system, since it amounts to about 2 per cent of total French taxes (including social security contributions).

Finally, it should be noted that, in terms of yield, the tax on developed land (IFB) is much more important than the tax on non-developed land (IFNB). The former yields four or five times more than the latter.

What is the weight of land taxation relative to the market value of land properties? In 1985, the communes' tax on non-developed land was around 1.2 per cent of the value of land. Adding the weight of the taxes raised by counties and regions, one would arrive at a total burden of about 1.5 per cent of market value. This is a high figure, relative to the yield of agricultural land in France, which is estimated to be about 3–5 per cent. Land taxes can therefore represent up to 50 per cent of land income. The effective rate of the tax is lower for the tax on developed land (IFB). For instance the effective rate of the communes' tax on residential property in 1985 was about 0.46 per cent of market value in 1985. Adding the counties' and regions' taxes bring this figure to about 0.60 per cent.

INTERCOMMUNAL DISPARITIES IN PROPERTY TAXATION

Taxes raised by local governments are 'unfair' in the sense that, whatever the tax base, some local governments are much better off than others. This can be documented in the case of the French local land taxes.

A preliminary question to be asked in this respect is: are the tax bases assessed identically in every commune? Otherwise, disparities in assessed tax bases could reflect differences in assessment between communes as much as differences in tax capacity. By and large, the answer to the question seems positive. Assessment (and collection) is basically the responsibility of the central government, and it is done by the county representative of the Ministry of Finance with the help of communal commissions. There is therefore a deliberate effort to unify assessment. To what extent it is successful is hard to say, in the absence of systematic studies relating assessed values to market values. There is probably a bias because of long time lags in reassessments. In between reassessment years, the assessed value of all properties is increased by a standard, identical figure. This means that properties whose value increases rapidly are relatively underestimated. However, this bias does not seem very important, and should not significantly alter our findings. For both taxes, differences in per capita bases are enormous. 'Rich' communes are *much* richer than 'poor' communes.

Table 8.3 Tax base disparities, 1987

	Tax on non-developed land (FF per head)	*Tax on developed land (FF per head)*
Average (m)	272[1]	3,617[2]
Standard deviation(s)	520	1,884
Coefficient of variation (s/m)	1.91	0.52
Maximum	4,041	16,810
Minimum	2	200
Max: min ratio	2,020:1	84:1

Notes:
1 FF 207 for France as a whole
2 FF 3,028 for France as a whole

These differences are in part explained by the size of communes. This is easy to understand for the tax on non-developed land: in general the smaller the commune is in terms of population, the more rural it is and the higher its per capita tax base is:

$$B_{nd} = \underset{(0.0020)}{-0.0108}\ S + \underset{(488)}{419} \qquad R^2 = 0.128$$

where B_{nd} is the per capita base of the tax on non-developed land (in francs) and S is the size of communes (number of inhabitants).

The reverse is true for the tax on developed land, although it is not so clear:

$$B_d = \underset{(0.0147)}{0.0404}\ S + \underset{(3{,}581)}{3{,}373} \qquad R^2 = 0.037$$

where B_d is the per capita base of the tax on developed land (in francs). What happens is that the per capita tax base first decreases with commune size, then increases. For larger communes, then, the tax base is positively correlated with size: the per capita value of buildings increases with commune size.

One would expect per capita tax bases to be related to per capita incomes, both because high income is generated by high land and building values, and because high income families have high value houses. As a matter of fact, there is a positive relationship, but it is rather weak:

$$B_{nd} = \underset{(0.033)}{0.0028\, I} + \underset{(534)}{169} \qquad R^2 = 0.0037$$

$$B_d = \underset{(0.082)}{0.0400\, I} + \underset{(13.282)}{3.256} \qquad R^2 = 0.0012$$

where I is per capita income.

Intercommunal disparities in land tax bases in France are therefore enormous, and erratic. As a matter of chance, a given commune may have a very low or a very high per capita tax base. This is true even if one limits the analysis to the less volatile tax on developed land, and to the large communes. For the 100 communes with more than 10,000 inhabitants in our sample, the minimum: maximum ratio of the per capita tax base is 1:18 and the coefficient of dispersion is about 0.6.

LOCAL GOVERNMENT BEHAVIOUR IN RESPECT OF PROPERTY TAXATION

Local authorities cannot do much about their tax bases. For sure, they can – and do – try to attract people and businesses in order to increase the tax base on developed land; but this can hardly apply to the tax on non-developed land. They could try to push assessments up or down, but this policy would run counter to the central government desire to unify assessment practices, and it is not reported to be pursued by communes. What local authorities really can manipulate are the tax rates. To study local government behaviour in property taxation is to study rate-setting.

There are, indeed, large intercommunal differences in land tax rates, as shown in Table 8.4. Each commune simultaneously sets two tax rates: the rate of the IFNB and the rate of the IFB. These two sets of rates are well correlated with the rates of the other two local taxes. This can easily be explained by historic reasons. Until 1980, the rates of the four main local taxes were mechanically linked (through a complex mechanism), and communes could only set one 'overall' tax rate. They are now free to set independent rates for the four taxes, but they have used this freedom with prudence and restraint.

Table 8.4 Tax rate[1] disparities, 1987

	Tax on non-developed land (%)	*Tax on developed land (%)*
Average (m)	47[2]	14[3]
Standard deviation (s)	28	6
Coefficient variation (s/m)	0.60	0.43
Maximum	145	33
Minimum	1.5	1
Max: min ratio	97:1	33:1

Notes:
1 Rates here are effective rates, equal to yields divided by bases
2 36 per cent for France as a whole
3 13 per cent for France as a whole

What variables could explain rates? A first possible explanatory variable is tax bases: the higher the (per capita) tax base, the lower the tax rate. This relationship holds, but it is not very strong:

$$R_{nd} = \underset{(0.000035)}{-0.00011}\ B_{nd} + \underset{(0.27)}{0.50} \qquad R^2 = 0.049$$

$$R_d = \underset{(0.0000032)}{-0.00001}\ B_d + \underset{(0.061)}{0.142} \qquad R^2 = 0.048$$

where R_{nd} is the tax rate on non-developed land (as a percentage) and R_d is the tax rate on developed land (as percentage).

In other words, there is a sort of 'income effect' at work. To a limited extent, communes compensate for lower tax bases by higher tax rates. As a result, disparities in tax yields – shown in Table 8.5 – are somewhat less than disparities in tax bases.

A second possible explanatory variable is the size of commune. In practice, correlation analysis shows no relationship between rates and size.

A third explanatory variable could be income. One might think that high income communes can afford higher tax rates. In reality, the reverse seems to be true: rates and income are negatively (and also loosely) associated:

$$R_{nd} = \underset{(0.26)}{0.78} - \underset{(0.0000016)}{0.0000079}\ I \qquad R^2 = 0.106$$

$$R_d = \underset{(0.05)}{0.24} - \underset{(0.00000034)}{0.00000256}\ I \qquad R^2 = 0.222$$

A final explanatory variable could be found in the political persuasions of the communes. For sixty-six large communes, the political affiliation of the mayor elected in 1983 (who set the rates for 1987) was noted, and the communes classified as 'left' or 'right'. Table 8.6 suggests that 'left' communes tend to set higher tax rates than 'right' communes.

Table 8.5 Tax yield disparities, 1987

	Tax on non-developed land (FF per head)	*Tax on developed land (FF per head)*
Average (m)	99[1]	490[2]
Standard deviation (s)	164	469
Coefficient of variation (s/m)	1.66	0.96
Maximum	1,430	6,098
Minimum	1	47
Max: min ratio	1,430:1	130:1

Notes:
1 FF 75 for France as a whole
2 FF 402 for France as a whole

Table 8.6 Tax rates by political affiliation, 1987

	'Left'	*'Right'*	*Total*
Tax on NDL			
average rate	56.1%	42.3%	50.0%
standard deviation	37.6%	28.8%	34.7%
maximum	144.8%	92.6%	144.8%
minimum	8.8%	1.5%	1.5
Tax on DL			
average rate	17.4%	14.2%	16.0%
standard deviation	4.8%	6.4%	5.8%
maximum	27.5%	27.3%	27.5%
minimum	7.9%	1.1%	1.1%
Number of communes	37	29	66

A multiple regression analysis can be conducted, based on the three above-mentioned variables that appear to have some explanatory power:

$$R_{nd} = \underset{(0.17)}{0.63} + \underset{(0.189)}{0.695}\ B_{nd} - \underset{(0.0001)}{0.001}\ I + \underset{(8.46)}{1.081}\ P \qquad R^2 = 0.318$$

$$R_d = \underset{(0.05)}{0.18} - \underset{(0.0001)}{0.002}\ B_d - \underset{(0.0001)}{0.0001}\ I - \underset{(1.203)}{0.058}\ P \qquad R^2 = 0.523$$

where P is a dummy variable for political affiliation ($P = 0$ for 'left' and 1 for 'right').

This analysis, conducted for the sixty-six communes for which data on political affiliation are available, confirms and modifies some of preceding findings. It suggests a different behaviour of communes *vis-à-vis* the two kinds of land tax. For the tax on non-developed land, rates are positively correlated with bases and inversely correlated with income. They are also higher in 'right' communes than in 'left' communes. For the tax on developed land, rates are inversely correlated with bases and with income, and are higher in 'left' communes.

These results are somewhat disappointing. Local government behaviour is not easily explained by three simple variables. Part of the explanation is that rates are not set for each tax in isolation. In deciding the rate of a given land tax, a local government also takes into account the tax bases of the three other main local taxes (the other land tax, the business tax, and the housing tax), and the rates that it can politically decide for these three other local taxes. A more complex model, that would explain the simultaneous determination of the four rates, would have to be developed.

CONCLUSION

Property taxes are generally considered as good local taxes. It is argued that differences in tax rates between jurisdictions do not induce important interjurisdictional displacements of tax bases, because the supply of property in a given jurisdiction is inelastic. It is further argued that land taxes make it possible for each local government to decide its own tax policy, and to offer packages of taxes and services (high taxes and high service levels, or low taxes and low service levels) between which citizens can choose.

These assertions are not borne out by our analysis of local property taxation in France. The main feature – largely ignored by most theorists – appears to be the very large interjurisdictional disparities in terms of tax bases. There are 'rich' communes, with high per capita tax bases, and 'poor' communes, with low per capita tax bases, and rich communes are many times richer than poor communes. These very large disparities are probably in part due to the small size of French communes, but disparities are very significant also between large communes (i.e. those with over 10,000 inhabitants).

In view of such large imbalances, the idea that communes can have policies and decide on tax-cum-services packages is not very realistic. In practice, communes attempt to correct, in part, for the imbalances, so poorer communes do have somewhat higher rates. But these corrections are grossly insufficient, and communes that are rich in terms of tax bases are also rich in terms of tax yields and, presumably, in terms of services offered.

It also appears that it is not really adequate to study local government tax behaviour in the case of only one (or two) taxes, namely land taxes. There are, in France, four main local taxes, and the rates of these taxes are not determined independently. They are jointly set by communes, taking into consideration historical and legal constraints, the tax bases of each tax, the political reactions to effective tax rates for each tax, and the levels of services financed by the taxes.

The large intercommunal disparities between tax bases and tax yields explain why commune taxes do not play a key role in the financing of local public services in France. First, many services (such as education) which are provided locally in many countries are provided and financed directly by the central government in France, on a more or less equal basis. Secondly, local taxes account for only about half of commune revenues in France, with central government subsidies of various sorts accounting for the other half. Since these subsidies are much more even, and in (a small) part inversely related to local tax bases, the disparities in per capita revenues between communes are much smaller than disparities in per capita local taxes. Thirdly, tax disparities between counties and regions are not as large as they are between communes, and this might explain the important, and increasing, role played by these levels of government in France.

9 Revealed preferences for local public goods

The Turin experiment

Stefano Piperno and Walter Santagata

TAKING FISCAL PREFERENCES SERIOUSLY[1]

This paper presents the initial results of an experimental attempt made in Turin to estimate a demand function for local public goods. The economic experiment carried out in Turin arose from the query 'is it possible to take individual preferences seriously in collective choices?' More precisely, what sense does this question make? The theory of social decisions, deriving from Arrow, suggests that any consistent method of aggregating individual preferences seems to lead to an extreme negation of individual preferences – i.e. to dictatorship. And representative democracies, however pluralistic they may be, seem unable to guarantee political representation of the general will: stronger groups invariably prevail. In either case, individual preferences are of no importance, at least until they become vested interests. Thus, taking fiscal preferences seriously requires, first of all, that they be given an identity and be revealed in ways that can be valued in terms of equity and efficiency. Secondly, it requires verification that individual preferences for public goods are substantially respected by the choices of local politicians and administrators charged with the planning of the public budget. Thirdly, it means making sense of the way these preferences are generated.

THE TURIN FISCAL EXPERIMENT

The fiscal and economic experiment carried out in Turin in 1986 was an attempt to induce a representative sample of inhabitants to reveal their preferences about the way local government manages economic resources. Six hundred and sixty-seven individuals over eighteen years of age were asked to take part in this experiment, which was very similar to a game. A questionnaire called 'If I were the Mayor . . .' was sent to each individual by post. In each envelope were two bar charts. These described the main per capita monetary accounts of the local budget, with revenues and expenditures in balance. Per capita monetary values were indicated for ten categories of expenditure and for four sources of revenue.

The expenditure categories were: street maintenance and lighting; registry offices; traffic control; sewerage and refuse collection; schools; nurseries; public transport; sport, parks and the arts; social welfare; and housing. The revenue categories were: direct taxes; indirect taxes; borrowing; and user charges.

The experiment was divided into three parts, representing, in order, a growing degree of specificity. The first step had a qualitative character: the respondents were asked to point out which categories they would like to modify to make the level of public services, or revenues, consistent with their personal preferences. They were able to reveal their qualitative preferences by putting +, – or = under the bars of the graphs representing each type of expenditure or revenue.

The second step was quantitative: the respondents were provided with monetary coupons that they could allocate among the various categories. The total per capita value of the budget was about Lit. 1.3m (about £700), and the total value of the coupons was 70 per cent of the total budget. The allocation procedure was quite simple: the respondent was asked to choose coupons reflecting his desired values and place them over the relevant bar (or bars) of the graphs. There were no 'free lunches'. If a person allocated a coupon in order to raise one category of expenditure, then it was necessary to reduce another category, or to increase one of the revenue sources by the same amount.

The third step allowed the individual citizen to specify choices in great detail. Options were expanded to a detailed list of the services included under each heading.

The experiment stopped here. Data on personal characteristics of the respondents, as well as their attitudes toward selected municipal services, were collected by means of a questionnaire.

THE MAIN RESULTS OF THE EXPERIMENT

Within the experiment the respondents were allowed to follow six different strategies. The actual individual choices were:

a No coupons used .... 7.5 per cent
b Expenditure structure modified without modifying the revenue structure .... 19.8 per cent
c Revenue structure modified without modifying the expenditure structure .... 0 per cent
d Both the expenditure and the revenue structure were modified, thus keeping the budget constant ..... 6.2 per cent
e Both total expenditure and total revenue were decreased .... 19.6 per cent
f Both total expenditure and total revenue were increased .... 46.9 per cent

As we can see the last strategy was the most preferred, followed in order of magnitude by the second and fifth. The results suggested that about 20 per cent of the respondents would have preferred a smaller (local) public sector, while a little less than 50 per cent would have preferred a larger public sector. The mean desired budget was 7 per cent less than the official budget for people who wanted it to be reduced, and 8 per cent more for those who wanted it increased. Of course, these values refer only to individual preferences; the way in which people coalesce and decide the size of the actual public budget through their voting and collective decision-making is a different matter. Indeed, none of the strategies had majority consent.

The quantitative analysis of coupon allocation allows us to say something about individual expenditure preferences, as shown in Table 9.1. Whereas, since the 1960s, municipalities have devoted most of their local resources to two kind of services – schools and public transport – the participants in our experiment no longer seemed to like this expenditure pattern. They required more expenditure on other services, such as refuse collection and sewerage, sport, parks and the arts, social welfare and housing.

To assess the 'distance' between individual preferences and the official budget (i.e. the potential level of political dissent) we have tried two different measurements. The more intuitive of these is the dispersion of individual values around the actual real value in each expenditure and revenue category.[2] This sort of variability around the official budget showed a mean 'distance' of about 17 per cent. However, this measure fails to capture the direction of the dissent. It does not reveal whether people dissent because they want more, less or the same level of public expenditures and revenues.

To establish the direction of such dissent, another more subjective measure has been created. Setting B_e as the actual expenditure and

Table 9.1 The Turin experiment: percentage difference between (average) desired budgets and actual budgets

Expenditure categories	%
Street maintenance and lighting	+11.9
Registry office	+7.4
Traffic control	−2.0
Sewerage and refuse collection	+5.6
Schools	0.0
Nurseries	−1.0
Public transport	−6.7
Sport, parks and the arts	+11.2
Social welfare	+14.8
Housing	+18.6
Income categories	
Direct taxes	+1.5
Indirect taxes	+0.5
Borrowing	+7.9
User charges	+4.9

revenue level, and setting B_i as the difference between B_e and an individual's preferred budget, then the measure

$$S = 1 - B_i/B_e$$

can serve as an index of dissent.

The index S has a positive sign when people dissent because they want a lower budget, and a negative sign when they dissent because they want a bigger budget. Given the aggregate value of the coupons is fixed at 70 per cent of the budget, S can vary between 0.7 and −0.7. The distribution of S is shown in Table 9.2.

Table 9.2 The Turin experiment: frequency distribution of S – a measure of dissent

S	*Frequency (%)*
−0.49 to −0.07	19.2
−0.07 to −0.03	18.9
−0.03 to 0.00	8.8
0.00	33.3
0.00 to 0.03	6.6
0.03 to 0.07	13.6

This indicator, S, fails to reveal the dissent of people who would only change the structure of the budget without changing its total value.

As we can see from Table 9.2, 33 per cent of the respondents did not modify the total value of the budget, whereas 20 per cent would have demanded its decrease and about 47 per cent its increase.

We would like to stress another important result relating to the implications of individual fiscal preferences for the design of tax policy. Respondents who prefer a larger public sector and more public expenditures reveal a preference for more borrowing (+7.9 per cent) and more charges (+4.9 per cent). Since the issue at hand is concerned with efficiency, the last figure reflects fiscal sophistication.

THE DEMAND FOR LOCAL PUBLIC GOODS

The vast empirical literature on the demand for local public goods can be surveyed in several different but overlapping ways. It is useful to refer briefly to the different approaches.

The earliest studies employed cross-sectional analyses of per capita local expenditures to analyse the determinants of local public expenditures. They explained differences among local communities in terms of a set of socio-economic and environmental variables, such as the degree of urbanisation, per capita income, absolute population size or its rate of growth, and various types of grants from higher levels of government. All of these studies are generally criticised as *ad hoc* explanations, in the sense that they are not derived from the rational choice theory, as reflected in public choice theory. Moreover, they do not distinguish clearly between the demand and supply sides (see Inman, 1979).

The distinctive feature of the second approach, which uses both micro and macro data and both quantitative and qualitative models, is that it derives a demand function for public goods from the constrained maximisation of individual utility functions. In turn, this field of research can be further divided. One approach is concerned with the estimation of a demand equation according to the traditional theory of the rational consumer (Birsdall, 1965, and Deacon, 1977); these studies are based on the hypothesis that public and private goods are interchangeable (see Gramlich and Rubinfeld, 1982). Another approach uses models of linear expenditure systems to estimate the demand for public goods (Stone, 1954, Deacon, 1978, Dudley and Montmarquette, 1981, and McGuire and Groth, 1985).

Some studies covered by this second approach try to incorporate individual demand for local expenditures in models of the political process through which individual preferences are aggregated. Usually these models are based on the median voter theory (Bowen, 1943, and Pommerehne and Frey, 1976). Consequently, their reliability depends on the validity of this model approximating actual political processes (see Borcherding and Deacon, 1972, and Bergstrom and Goodman, 1973). More complex political issues are faced in the so-called 'dominant party' model (Henderson, 1968, Inman, 1971 and 1979, and Romer and Rosenthal, 1979). The dynamic of this model is a two-party struggle for office, from which a clear and controlling winner emerges. In contrast to the median voter model, political parties are the crucial agents and individual voters have scant influence. The model is best suited for the analysis of mutli-service government in medium-to-large cities. A typical example of a 'dominant party' is the Democratic party in New York City. In other studies covered by this second approach, the demand for public goods was derived from an economic experiment which tried to overcome the free-rider problem and allow participants to reveal their true demands (Isaac, McCue and Plott, 1985, and Schneider and Pommerehne, 1981).

The third approach to the demand for local public goods is more difficult to define. It is a sort of social science approach, which grows out of the cross-fertilisation of ideas among the disciplines of economics, politics, psychology and sociology. Although it does not contradict previous approaches, the aim of this kind of study is to investigate the influence of taxpayer attitudes on tax and public expenditure issues (Lewis, 1983). The main tools of analysis of this approach are opinion polls, surveys and economic experiments, generally based on micro data (see, for instance, Mueller, 1963, Schmolders, 1970, and Strumpel, 1969). In the United States, the Advisory Commission on Intergovernmental Relations (ACIR) has, since 1971, conducted an annual public opinion poll about public attitudes toward government and taxes. More recently, mainly in the United States, many studies have attempted to find out the causes of the so-called fiscal revolt and the tax limitation movements, after the passage of Proposition 13 by a referendum in the State of California in 1978 (Citrin, 1979, David, 1980, and Courant, Gramlich and Rubinfeld, 1980).

Many of these third approach studies are also based on rational consumer theory and simple voting models, as in the previous approaches, but much stress is placed upon socio-economic variables other than income and tax price, such as age, sex, family size, level of education, and the occupation of respondents, to improve the performance of the models used. In some ways we can say that this approach reflects 'bounded rationality models' which try to insert realistic hypotheses about consumer behaviour – such as lack of information and non-rationality – into the conventional approach.

We can also mention two other contributions, from which we have drawn the idea for our experiment. These are Strauss and Hughes (1976), who carried out a survey in North Carolina, and Hockley and Harbour (1983) who carried out a survey in England and Wales. Each survey was based on a questionnaire which permitted respondents to make hypothetical expenditure and tax recommendations with transferable penny coupons. Unlike our experiment, however, the coupons were not subjected to the budget constraint.

The fourth main approach to estimating demand functions for public goods is the hedonic approach, based on market methods. This indirect method consists of estimating the implicit price of a public good (such as clean air) by reference to differential prices in markets for private goods. For instance, differences in the selling prices of houses located in different areas with different degrees of air pollution can be interpreted as a reflection of the willingness to pay for clean air, when all the other relevant factors are taken into account (see Brookshire *et al.*, 1982).

QUANTITATIVE VERSUS. QUALITATIVE RESPONSE MODELS OF THE DEMAND FOR LOCAL PUBLIC GOODS

In the light of the political and socio-economic models outlined above, we assume that, given the lack of reliable data about tax prices, the fiscal preferences of citizens can best be explained in terms of income and a series of political and socio-economic variables.

We will present, estimate and compare two models, the first concerned with quantitative response variables and the second with qualitative response variables. Both the models deal with the same set of independent variables, which can be placed into five main groups as outlined below.

Economic and fiscal variables

The first variable in this group is *INCOME*. Generally the income elasticity of the demand for public goods is expected to be positive, with a value that varies from 0 to 1 or more, depending on the particular behavioural hypothesis and the characteristics of the particular public good in question. Family income, as declared in the questionnaire, has been weighted on the basis on the consumption patterns of families of different size, transforming it into individual incomes.

The second variable in this group is termed INDEX and has been constructed to reflect attitudes toward the tax system, as orientated either toward redistributive goals (equity) or efficiency (the benefit principle). We assume that those who are redistribution-orientated will order the revenue alternatives in the sequence 1 borrowing, 2 direct taxes, 3 indirect taxes, and 4 user charges, whereas those who are efficiency-orientated will reverse this ordering.

As a first approximation we constructed the index as follows:

$$\textit{INDEX} = Var1+0.5Var2-0.5Var3-Var4$$

where *Var*1 = the ratio of the proposed variation in borrowing to actual borrowing, *Var*2 = the ratio of the proposed variation in direct taxes to actual direct taxes, *Var*3 = the ratio of the proposed variation in indirect taxes to actual indirect taxes, and *Var*4 = the ratio of the proposed variation in charges to the actual level of charges. The two intermediate sources of finance – direct and indirect taxes – are assigned weights less than unity because of their ambiguity. The index has a negative value if the attitude is pro-efficiency, and a positive value if it is pro-redistribution.

The third and final variable in this group is termed SQMET. This equals the size of home in square meters for home-owners. This variable has been constructed multiplying the home size by a dummy variable: this has the value of 1 for owners and 0 for non-owners.

Personal variables

There are five variables in this group, as follows:

Sex

This is a dummy variable with 1 = male and 0 = female.

Age

This is measured in years.

Education

This variable consists of a set of dummies reflecting the various levels attained: OBBL = primary and secondary school; SUPE = high school;

and GRADU = graduated. Thus the constant captures the differential preferences of less-educated people.

Employment

This variable also consists of a set of dummies indicating labour force participation: AUTON = self-employed workers; DIPENI = white collar workers; DIPEN2 = blue collar workers; RETIR = retired people; and OUT = non-active people, excluding retired.

Region of birth

This variable identifies people born in Piedmont and people born in the south of Italy. The choice of this variable makes sense because of the importance of migration to Turin from the South during the 1950s and 1960s. Social research in this area has documented deep cultural differences between people from the southern regions and people born in Piedmont. Again, variables are dummies – PIEM = people born in Piedmont, and SOUTH = people born in southern Italy. To try to capture multiplicative effects, we multiplied them by years of residence in Turin in the single category regressions. More precisely, PIEMAN is people from Piedmont by years of residence, and MERAN is people from southern regions by years of residence. Consequently, the constant captures the effect of other regions off origin.

Family structure variables

There is no doubt about the importance of family structure. The demand by an individual household for particular public services is related to the number and age of the people living in the household. We constructed six typologies: SINGLE = one-person households; COUPLE = households with two people, both under 55 years; COUPLEO = households with two people over 55 years; FAM = 1425 = households with more than two people including one or more children between 14 and 25 years; and FAM025 = households with more than two people and one or more children between 0 and 25 years. In testing the model, however, these variables were reduced to four: SINGLE = one-person households; COUPLE = two-person households; FAMWCHIL = families with children under 25 years; and FAMOTHER = other families.

Political variables

Preferences can be influenced by political factors. The influence of party affiliation has been estimated by using a dummy – *left* – which indicates a vote in favour of the leftist coalition that governed Turin from 1975 until 1985, after which a centre-left coalition without the Communist Party took over. This variable reflects ideological perspectives such as, for instance, the acceptance of redistributive policies.

Public goods consumption

The final variable used is called *USE* and is a sort of index of public goods consumption, constructed as a sum of indicators of use of some public services, namely public transport, nursery and elementary schools, libraries, theatres, sports facilities and parks. The indicator consists of a set of dummies, with values of 1 for users and 0 for non-users. We are aware of the need to improve the quality of this variable, which does not weight the importance of various services, and we are trying to create a monetary index, capable of measuring the benefits citizens obtain from local public expenditures.

THE QUANTITATIVE SOCIO-ECONOMIC CHOICE MODEL

The model we have estimated is a traditional utility-maximising model with its solution derived through maximisation subject to a budget constraint. Previous hypotheses and the specification of variables suggests two further considerations.

First, starting from a multiplicative specification of the utility function, we have estimated an additive logarithmic demand function:

$$\log X = \log c + \alpha \log Y + \beta \text{ Index} + \alpha \text{ Individual Tastes}$$

where X is expenditure on the local public good, Y is individual income, Index is an appropriate measure of tax-price and c is a constant. Secondly, auxiliary variables are introduced to take account of differences in individual tastes. Each respondent household was classified on the basis of its personal variables, its family structure variables, its political variables and its public goods consumption variables.

In our experiment people revealed their fiscal preferences by allocating monetary coupons. Thus we have an almost continuously valued variable that represents individual choices for the desired budget.

Moreover, the value is the direct result of the experimental design and is superior to quantitative measures used in other studies. For instance, Gramlich and Rubinfeld (1982) used in their study a quantitative variable that reflected the whole local budget, increased or decreased by 5, 10, 15, or 20 per cent or more. Hockley and Harbour (1983) define, as response variables, the allocated coupons. In their context the *deus ex machina* coupons could be used only to increase expenditures or to decrease revenues. The budget constraint in that analysis has no real sense. In contrast, our dependent variable is the preferred individual budget. It is the result of various possible strategies and allows the respondents a great flexibility, given the budget constraint.

The 'desired budget' column in Table 9.3 presents the estimated parameters of the quantitative model. Overall, the model runs in a satisfactory way. Ten of the coefficients differ from zero at a level of significance of at least 10 per cent.

Because a large number of dummy variables are used, the *INTERCEPT* term represents a special type of respondent. We can think of such a respondent. This individual is female, illiterate and of neither Piedmontese nor Southern Italian origin. She votes against the majority coalition. She is not the owner of her home, where she lives without a husband. In all likelihood, she is a self-employed worker.

As far as the economic variables are concerned, the variable has the expected positive sign, indicating that the desired budget is greater the more redistribution-orientated the respondents. The effect of an increase in the individual income is positively correlated with the desired budget. The elasticity of the desired budget with respect to the mean income is 0.02. In contrast, being a home-owner is a condition that negatively influences the desired budget. Moreover, the larger the home (in terms of square metres), the greater the disagreement with the official budget.

Among the social variables, it is worth noting that men prefer lower budgets than women and that the level of education has a positive effect on the desired budget. Also, retirement implies a higher demand for public goods. And people from Piedmont who have lived in Turin for many years have a higher desired budget than people born in other regions of Italy.

As far as the political variables are concerned, electoral support for the Socialist and Communist ruling coalition implies an ideological bent towards a greater welfare state. Thus the sign of the variable *LEFT* is positive, as expected. Turning to public goods consumption, the more people tend to use local public goods, the higher their demands.

Table 9.3 The Turin experiment: general regression results

Independent variables	*Desired budget*	A_1 *(more expenditure)*	B_1 *(less expenditure)*	P_1 *(no change)*
	(t in parentheses)	(χ^2 in parentheses)	(χ^2 in parentheses)	(χ^2 in parentheses)
INTERCEPT	7.01 (106.5)	−5.03 (9.8)	−2.3 (1.4)	5.6 (10.1)
INCOME	0.022 (2.37)***	0.54 (5.8)***	0.07 (0.08)	−0.7 (8.0)***
INDEX	0.04 (3.6)***	0.93 (12.4)***	−0.44 (2.07)**	−0.77 (7.26)***
SEX	−0.014 (1.74)***	−0.01 (0.01)	0.3 (1.7)	−0.2 (1.3)
OBBL	0.022 (1.53)**	0.33 (0.9)	0.5 (1.8)	−0.7 (4.3)***
SUPE	0.028 (1.7)***	0.20 (0.2)	−0.07 (0.08)	−0.12 (0.09)
GRADU	0.008 (0.38)	0.33 (0.4)	−0.43 (0.44)	−0.04 (0.01)
MERAN	0.0002 (1.1)	−0.003 (0.6)	0.007 (2.5)**	−0.002 (0.37)
PIEMAN	0.0004 (2.3)***	0.003 (0.67)	−0.003 (0.49)	−0.001 (0.12)
SQMET	−0.0001 (1.8)***	−0.003 (4.1)***	−0.00003 (0.0)	0.004 (5.01)***
DIPENI	−0.005 (0.3)	0.66 (4.19)***	0.49 (1.5)	−1.08 (10.1)***
DIPEN2	0.02 (1.2)	0.87 (6.47)***	−0.27 (0.4)	−0.7 (4.2)***
OUT	0.006 (0.4)	0.59 (3.07)	0.24 (0.3)	−0.7 (5.3)***
RETIR	0.02 (1.4)**	1.01 (8.8)***	−0.15 (0.1)	−0.9 (7.7)***
USE	0.001 (1.6)**	0.04 (7.6)***	−0.004 (0.05)	−0.05 (7.7)***
LEFT	0.01 (1.7)***	0.47 (6.4)***	−0.22 (0.9)	−0.37 (3.4)***
COUPLE	0.004 (0.6)	0.21 (0.4)	−0.08 (0.04)	−0.15 (0.19)
FAMWCHILD	0.01 (0.7)	0.08 (0.06)	−0.36 (0.7)	0.18 (0.2)
FAMOTHER	0.007 (0.6)	0.14 (0.2)	0.20 (0.3)	−0.31 (1.6)
	F: 2.56 R^2: 0.04 No of cases 607			

Fraction of concordant pairs of predicted probabilities and responses =	0.65	0.60	0.66
Rank correlation between predicted probability and response	0.33	0.24	0.36

Level of significance: *** 0–5% ** 5–10%

THE QUALITATIVE SOCIO-ECONOMIC CHOICE MODEL

Many studies based on qualitative response variables use logit or probit models to predict the probability that certain events will occur. As a practical matter, dichotomous variables are poorer, in terms of embedded information, than continuously-valued variables. Our experiment allows us, too, to estimate a qualitative response model.

Qualitative dependent variables are represented by dichotomous values of desired expenditures: they assume the value of 1 if the respondent wants more expenditure and 0 if he or she prefers less expenditure or no change. To explain the total desired budget (without looking at expenditure categories) we shall define the probability of increasing the budget (A_1), the probability of decreasing the budget (B_1), and the probability of not modifying the budget (P_1) as our response variables.

For the qualitative dependent variables we shall adopt a choice model that indicates the probability of modifying the total budget. We can observe a dummy variable, Y, defined by $Y=1$ if people want the total budget to increase and $Y=0$ otherwise. The logit model will be used (see Maddala, 1983). Such a model allows us to estimate the contribution of several variables to the probability that an action will be taken, that is that $\Pr(Y = 1)$.

The assumption of this binary model is that P_i, or $\Pr(Y=1)$, in our case the probability that the total budget will be increased, is based on the cumulative logistic probability function:

$$\Pr(Y=1) = P_i = 1/(1+\exp(-Z_i)) \tag{1}$$

where:

$$Z_i = a + bX_i \tag{2}$$

From (1), transforming and taking logarithms we obtain,

$$Z_i = \log(P_i / (1-P_i)) \tag{3}$$

Thus,

$$\log(P_i / (1-P_i)) = a+bX_i \tag{4}$$

is the equation to be estimated.

The results of the estimated logit model are presented the last three columns of Table 9.3. We first examine the probability of an increase in the desired budget (A_1). The model chi-square is significant at more than 99 per cent. The rate of correct predicted choices is 65 per cent and the rank correlation between predicted probability and response is 0.33.

All the significant variables have the same sign as those estimated in the quantitative model. The problem is that with a dichotomous dependent variable, which provides poorer information, and with a confidence level of 90 per cent for rejection of the null hypothesis, the logit model estimates that the parameters of four variables which are significant in the quantitative model do not differ significantly from zero; and it adds two variables that are not significant in the quantitative model. The extra significant variables are the characteristics of being white-collar or blue-collar workers, each of which has a positive sign.

However, the logit specification does permit us to separate three possible strategies: to increase (equation A_1), to decrease (equation B_1) or to maintain the actual level of the total budget (P_1). And the different specification of the model is of great interest. In fact, the logistic function allows us to take account of the fact that constant changes in the independent variables generally produce a lower change in the response variable as it approaches 0 or 1.

The second equation (B_1), focusing on the probability of reducing the official budget, produces very poor results. Only two variables are significant at a level of confidence between 90 and 95 per cent. For the index variable, the sign changes, as expected. In the equation P_1, on the other hand, almost all the variables have negative signs.

THE DEMANDS FOR SPECIFIC CATEGORIES OF EXPENDITURE

We have also tried to estimate quantitative models for specific categories of expenditure. In this first attempt we aggregated some categories into more general ones: thus 'basic services' include registry offices, traffic control and sewerage and refuse collection, while 'education' includes schools and nurseries. Public transport, sport,

Table 9.4 Regression results with the single categories as dependent variables

Independent variables	*Dependent variables*						
	Basic services	*Education*	*Transport*	*Sport parks arts*	*Social services*	*Housing*	*Education (only high level)*
INTERCEPT	276.211	319.894	378.859	95.426	143.834	112.041	340.684
	(13.876)	(14.785)	(21.440)	(9.107)	(12.609)	(11.538)	(23.828)
INCOME	.0031	.0079	.0165**	.0039	.0059	−.004	.016**
	(.0061)	(.0066)	(.009)	(.0039)	(.0057)	(.005)	(.009)
INDEX	8.830***	15.170***	12.033**	−.242	7.219**	10.658***	15.001**
	(4.635)	(4.875)	(6.905)	(2.904)	(4.285)	(3.999)	(9.223)
SEX	−5.041	−7.121**	2.702	−.910	−2.684	1.218	−8.106
	(3.771)	(4.080)	(5.771)	(2.409)	(3.568)	(3.261)	(8.200)
AGE	−.144	−.164	−.020	−.124	.048	−.091	−.550
	(.159)	(.167)	(.239)	(.101)	(.147)	(.136)	(.345)
MERAN	−.185***	.101	.142	−.014	.039	.016	.262
	(.081)	(.089)	(.124)	(.052)	(.077)	(.070)	(.197)
PIEMAN	.0011	.134	.165	.0012	.040	−.050	.163
	(.083)	(.089)	(.126)	(.053)	(.078)	(.072)	(.168)
OBBL	17.077***	3.946	−8.478	6.444	12.882***	1.330	–
	(6.873)	(7.782)	(10.530)	(4.587)	(6.503)	(5.937)	
SUPE	13.499**	8.380	−7.543	6.123	7.711	3.570	–
	(8.322)	(9.195)	(12.563)	(5.466)	(7.736)	(7.107)	–

GRADU	11.549	3.326	−9.003	−.384	−.037	10.949	–
	(10.251)	(11.180)	(15.323)	(6.626)	(9.511)	(8.790)	
AUTON	9.450	6.054	−18.079**	9.281***	−1.880	−7.937	17.916
	(7.030)	(7.584)	(10.802)	(4.475)	(6.690)	(6.091)	(15.571)
DIPEN1	−1.660	−.764	−5.518	−2.840	2.150	2.318	10.584
	(5.647)	(6.001)	(8.659)	(3.543)	(5.259)	(4.862)	(10.653)
DIPEN2	4.028	7.678	7.319	3.180	−7.457	1.265	−10.633
	(5.824)	(6.228)	(9.085)	(3.664)	(5.442)	(4.997)	(24.270)
RETIR	2.599	8.206	7.771	−1.357	2.807	4.724	40.881***
	(6.240)	(6.746)	(9.494)	(4.031)	(5.906)	(5.407)	(19.023)
SQMET	−.006	–	–	–	–	−.791**	–
	(.057)					(.099)	
OWNER	−3.979	.014	−.769	.115	−4.047	−6.133**	−16.859***
	(3.683)	(3.925)	(5.523)	(2.324)	(3.422)	(3.153)	(8.330)
SINGLE	−12.804**	−4.140	−8.847	−2.231	−6.676	7.557	−26.541
	(7.951)	(8.578)	(12.831)	(5.078)	(7.439)	(7.637)	(18.547)
COUPLE	2.449	−4.971	10.596	−7.711**	−5.802	−1.162	−24.485
	(6.924)	(7.496)	(10.723)	(4.478)	(6.553)	(5.981)	(16.422)
FAMWCHIL	−13.064***	−5.071	5.211	−2.580	−.327	2.649	−14.063
	(6.366)	(6.960)	(9.722)	(4.139)	(6.032)	(5.489)	(14.198)
USE	703	–	–	–	–	–	–
	(1.112)						
SPORT	–	3.062		2.671	–		2.253
		(4.570)		(2.692)			(9.183)
LIBR	–	1.909	–	.285	–		7.078
	–	(4.651)		(2.759)			(8.670)

MUSEUMS	–	5.357 (4.223)	–	−1.182 (2.553)	–		.383 (8.117)
TRANSP	–	–	13.616** (7.374)		–		
NOSCHOOL		−19.698** (11.083)					−69.558*** (25.599)
CAR	–	–	−10.679 (8.126)		–		
CULT1	–	–	–	1.089 (2.611)	–		
CULT2	–	–	–	9.224*** (2.688)			
PARKS				.137 (2.562)			
REDLEC	–	4.778*** (.971)	–		–		7.308*** (2.043)
REDRIS	–	–	–	1.236 (.784)			
F	2.179**	2.751**	1.356	2.430**	.994	1.799**	2.633**
R^2	.06(.03)	.09(.06)	.04(.01)	.09(.05)	.02(.00)	.05(.02)	.22(.14)
No. of cases	597	594	604	592	604	597	190

Notes:
1 Standard errors are shown in parentheses; for the meaning of the variables see the text.
2 Level of significance: ** 5–10% ***0–5%
3 Adjusted R^2 in parentheses

parks and the arts, social welfare and housing have instead been estimated individually. For these estimates we used some new variables, defined below:

NOSCHOOL: number of children not using a state school.
PROPI: 0= non-owner of home; 1= owner.
SPORT: 1= user of sport facilities (the respondent or some household members); 0= non-user.
LIBR: 1= user of public libraries (the respondent or some household members); 0= non-user.
MUSEUMS: 1= user; 0= non-user.
TRANSP: 1= user of public transport (the respondent, or some household members); 0= non-user.
PARKS: 1= park user (the respondent or some household members); 0= non-user.
CAR: 1= owner of car; 0= non-owner.
REDSC: Sum of positive responses for the financing of some educational services with user charges.
REDLEIS: Sum of positive responses for the financing of some leisure services (theatres, visual arts etc.) with user charges.
CULTI: 1= user of theatres, opera and concert houses; 0= non-user.
CULT2: 1= user of some performing arts run by the municipality; 0= non-user.

The results of this analysis – which uses a linear model – are shown in Table 9.4. Basic services are positively and significantly related to the level of education, and negatively to SOUTH, FAMWCHIL, and SINGLE. One-person households and families with children are probably more concerned with other services, such as education, parks and housing, although the results of the other equations do not confirm this hypothesis. Income is not significant.

Educational services are positively and significantly related to INDEX, REDSC, SEX (females), and negatively to NOSCHOOL. The presence of nursery schools among the services may explain the interest of females, due to their increased participation in the labour market.

The next equation estimated is concerned with recreational services (sport, parks, arts). Our hypothesis is that these are services with regressive fiscal incidence, meaning that their distribution is positively related to income (i.e. these services have benefits that are pro-rich). Unfortunately the income parameter is not significantly different from zero. It must be noted, nevertheless, that self-employed workers (who may be relatively rich) ask for more services of this kind. Use of services (CULT2) and redistributive attitudes (REDRIS) are both positively related to the desired expenditures. Families without children are not concerned with services of this kind.

Housing services are negatively related to the size of homes and to home ownership. On the other hand, there is a positive relationship with redistributive attitude. Indeed, the fact that this variable enters all the equations for particular expenditure categories with the same sign should be stressed. The transport services and social services equations produce poor results, as indicated by the low value obtained in the *F* test.

At this stage of the research, we can only point out how difficult it is to explain the demand for particular local public expenditures in general terms. More work is needed, probably splitting our sample into more homogeneous categories of individuals by factors such as levels of education, age and type of job.

CONCLUSIONS

In general, the predominance of positive signs among the parameters estimated – both in the quantitative response model and in the logit analysis for the probability of an increase in the official budget – corroborates the relevant demand for local public goods already noted when the data were examined in a descriptive way. Moreover, the general positive relationship with variables that are supposed to increase as social and economic development proceeds (such as income and education) suggests future growth in the demand for public goods. The latter conclusion, of course, might be vitiated by shifts in fiscal preferences – the INDEX variable – and by shifts in political preferences – the LEFT variable. To take account of such changes, the case for a political and socio-economic approach to an explanation of the public budget, as compared with the simple rational consumer model, seems well founded. Turning to the specific budget categories, we can only point out the relevance of redistributive aspects of local public expenditures. Attitudes toward redistribution and the use of public goods seem to be good predictors of desired expenditures. It thus seems clear that any forecast of future trends in outlays must reflect the evolution of redistributive conflicts in our society.

NOTES

1 The sources of data are drawn from Santagata and Marchese (1986). A first version of this paper was presented at the Conference of the European Public Choice Society, held in Reggio Calabria, April 1987. We would like to thank D. Mueller, A. Peacock and E. Zimmermann for the useful suggestions they gave us at that conference. Thanks are also due to H. Hochman for helpful comments on the previous version of this paper.

2 The dissent variable is the square root of the sum of the squared deviations between desired revenues or expenditures (s^* and e^*) and actual revenues or expenditures (s and e), divided by the number of issues (14) i.e. ($(s^*-s)^2 + (e^*-e)^2$)/14.

REFERENCES

Bergstrom, T.C. and Goodman, R.P. (1973), 'Private demands for public goods', *American Economic Review* 63:3.

Birdsall, W.C. (1965), 'A study of the demand for public goods', in R.A. Musgrave (ed.) *Essays in Fiscal Federalism*, Washington DC: Brookings Institution.

Borcherding T.E. and Deacon R.T. (1972) 'The demand for the services of non-federal governments', *American Economic Review* 62:5.

Bowen, H.R. (1943) 'The interpretation of voting in the allocation of economic resources', *Quarterly Journal of Economics* 58:1.

Brookshire, D.S., Thayer, M.A., Schulze, W.D., and d'Arge R.C., (1982) 'Valuing public goods: a comparison of survey and hedonic approaches', *American Economic Review* 72:3.

Citrin, J. (1979) 'Do people want something for nothing? Public opinion in taxes and government spending', *National Tax Journal* 32:2, supplement.

Courant, P.N., Gramlich, E.M. and Rubinfeld D.C. (1980) 'Why voters support tax limitation amendments: the Michigan case', *National Tax Journal* 33:3.

David, M. (1980) *Citizens' Views of Taxation and Tax Reform for Wisconsin*, State of Wisconsin: Madison.

Deacon, R.T. (1977) 'Private choice and collective outcomes: evidence from public sector demand analysis', *National Tax Journal* 30:4.

Deacon, R.T. (1978) 'A demand model for the local public sector' *Review of Economics and Statistics* 60:2.

Dudley, L. and Montmarquette, C. (1981) 'The demand for military expenditures: an international comparison', *Public Choice* 37:1.

Gramlich, E.M. and Rubinfeld, D.L. (1982) 'Micro estimates of public spending demand functions and tests of the Tiebout and median-voter hypotheses', *Journal of Political Economy* 90:3.

Henderson, J.M. (1968) 'Local government expenditures: a social welfare analysis', *Review of Economics and Statistics* 50:2.

Hockley, G.C. and Harbour, G. (1983) 'Revealed preferences between public expenditures and taxation cuts: public sector choice', *Journal of Public Economics* 22:3.

Inman, R.P. (1971) 'Towards an econometric model of local budgeting' in *Proceedings of the 64th Annual Conference on Taxation* Lexington: National Tax Association.

Inman, R.P. (1979) 'The fiscal performance of local governments: an interpretation review' in P. Mieszkowski and M. Straszheim, *Current Issues in Urban Economics* Baltimore: Johns Hopkins University Press.

Isaac, R.M., McCue, K.F. and Plott, C.R. (1985) 'Public goods provision in an experimental environment', *Journal of Public Economics* 26:1.

Lewis, A. (1983) *The Psychology of Taxation*, Oxford: Martin Robertson.

Maddala, G.S. (1983) *Limited-Dependent and Qualitative Variables in Econometrics*, Cambridge: Cambridge University Press.

McGuire, M.C. and Groth, C.M.Jr (1985) 'A method for identifying the public goods allocation process within a group', *Quarterly Journal of Economics* 100: supplement.

Mueller, E. (1963) 'Public attitudes toward fiscal programs', *Quarterly Journal of Economics* 77:2.

Pommerehne, W.W. and Frey, B.S. (1976) 'Two approaches to estimating public expenditures', *Public Finance Quarterly* 4:4.

Romer, T. and Rosenthal, H. (1979) 'Bureaucrats vs. voters: on the political economy of resource allocation by direct democracy', *Quarterly Journal of Economics* 93:4.

Santagata, W. and Marchese, C. (1986) *Se Io Fossi il Sindaco . . . Le Preferenze Fiscali Prese Sul Serio*, IRES Working Paper 74.

Schmolders, G. (1970) 'Survey research in public finance: a behavioural approach to fiscal policy', *Public Finance* 25:2.

Schneider, F. and Pommerehne, W.W. (1981) 'Free riding and collective action: an experiment in public microeconomics', *Quarterly Journal of Economics* 46:4.

Stone, R.D. (1954) 'Linear expenditure systems and demand analysis: an application to the pattern of British demand', *Economic Journal* 64:3.

Strauss, R.P. and Hughes, D.G. (1976) 'A new approach to the demand for public goods', *Journal of Public Economics* 6:3.

Strumpel, B. (1969), 'The contribution of survey research to public finance' in A.T. Peacock (ed.), *Quantitative Methods in Public Finance*, New York: Praeger.

10 Business collective action and the role of local government in economic development

Robert J. Bennett and John Sellgren

INTRODUCTION

This paper focuses on the question of the ownership and management of business in relation to the economic development needs of local communities. Ownership is approached through two primary agencies: private sector independent businesses and local government. We do not raise the general issue of business ownership, but discuss the conditions under which individual businesses may wish to exercise wider social responsibilities, act collectively with each other, and join with local government, local economic initiatives, or other institutions. This discussion leads in turn to seeking a definition of the boundary between individual business action and the role of the different sectors in undertaking economic development within local communities.

Local economic development is defined in this context as a subnational action, taking place within the context of a local labour market and often covering an area greater than one local government jurisdiction, but with activity focused on the specific problems of locations requiring development or regeneration. Economic development is concerned with wealth creation, questions of employment, and the distribution of economic activities. The actors involved often include local government, but we focus attention also on the extensive network of private sector bodies, corporate social responsibility units, venture capital funds, enterprise agencies and enterprise boards. The field is, therefore, one characterised by a pluralism of agencies and approaches. We focus attention here on three main questions, as follows:

a What is the rationale for collective action by businesses and local government in local economies and what are the boundaries between the two?

b What are the forms and structures of projects which are being developed in Britain?
c What does current experience tell us about future policy actions in this field?

THE RATIONALE FOR COLLECTIVE ACTION

Public choice theory provides the most direct route to understanding business collective action in the economic development field. This theory suggests that firms taking collective action will form 'clubs' where their service demands can be satisfied by joint action (Buchanan, 1965). Such clubs may be sectoral or formed by other special interests, but frequently they are local clubs within a small group of sites or within a local labour market. The objectives are maximisation of benefits and minimisation of costs by collective as opposed to individual action. Benefits are to be gained in proportion to the level of joint externalities of each business and the level of spill-overs. Costs will derive chiefly from the direct costs of collaboration (such as administration and management costs) and the extent to which collective programmes involve support for actions which would be individually inappropriate but are necessary to obtain gains elsewhere. Clearly collective actions based on this approach will differ in scale depending upon the form of jointness and the costs involved, and there may be different levels of involvement for different collective objectives (see Buchanan, 1971 and 1975). This may also embrace different geographical scales: neighbourhood, local government unit, region and nation.

As the geographical scale of collective needs increases, and as the scale of the requirements also increases, it is likely that businesses by their own action will not be able to provide for collective needs. It is at this point that local government and other actors assume importance. We can thus recognise a hierarchy of economic development possibilities ranging from the firm's internal business policy, through its collective action, to government activity.

The chief motives for *internal* action by businesses, and the main contributions a firm can make to economic development, are to remain competitive to retain and expand business, and to continue growing. In this way a business makes a major contribution to the creation of wealth in the local and national economy through wages, direct and indirect employment, and local and central taxes, as well as through the production and sale of its goods and services. Internal action therefore emphasises effective management, investment and marketing.

Many businesses, however, widen their internal view beyond pure investment and marketing objectives towards a broader set of policies of 'social responsibility' or even 'altruism' in employment, trading and local 'neighbourhood' relations: primarily, therefore, performing as 'good corporate citizens'. They see it as in their long-term interest to be involved with local communities, to be seen to be taking action and to be 'progressive' and socially responsible. Self-interest remains a key aspect of this: fear of antti-industrial attitudes, a desire to improve the image of the firm or of business as a whole, good public and employee relations, or fear that if business does not take a lead then government will.

Beyond internal action many businesses act either independently or participate in collective activities, *external* to their main requirements.

Individual activities involve a widening of the 'good citizenship' policies internal to the firm so that a wider and stronger link to the local community is developed (see BiC, 1986, and Davies, 1988). Key examples are as follows:

Support for activities by local individuals and groups

This can take the form of donations of money and gifts in kind, such as transport vehicles and facilities, or it may take the form of promoting welfare, cultural, heritage and environmental activities; sometimes this support may be set as a percentage of profits (as in per cent clubs).

Location and investment

Sound investment projects can be supported in more disadvantaged areas – such as inner cities or declining regions – rather than on greenfield sites in order to provide employment and other benefits; financial institutions may make services available at a preferential cost, perhaps as 'soft loans', in order to help disadvantaged groups or localities.

Employment and training

Recruitment policy can be targeted to favour disadvantaged groups or localities; this can be combined with or separate from training and work experience programmes, and may extend to making available surplus training capacity, premises or facilities for local community use.

Purchasing policy

Sub-contracting and purchasing can be a major stimulus to the local economy, particularly if supplemented by early warning of requirements to new businesses and community business ventures. 'Meet the buyer' events, counselling and advice, expansion of tender lists, and diffusion of information, can all be used to stimulate local business activity.

Involvement in public affairs

Staff and management can play important roles in community and local life, for instance by membership of school governing bodies and curriculum support groups, area health boards and voluntary organisations – such membership can provide business expertise and perhaps some financial support; alternatively firms can second staff to bodies such as other local businesses (particularly start-ups and small firms), community projects, training schemes and specialist investment agencies to provide specialist skills.

Collective activities go beyond the individual links of single businesses to community agents or actors, and involve several businesses acting in conjunction with each other. Collective action is commonly based on individual interests and may represent an attempt to overcome market failure without public sector involvement. It is natural for businesses to seek or establish an appropriate agency to manage the larger resources and the collective range of priorities that arise when firms act together. The major potential vehicles are:

a Trade associations: these promote collective sectoral action.
b Chambers of commerce, local employer networks and business clubs: these promote collective action at the local community level.
c Community business schemes: these promote the collective organisation of donations.
d Enterprise Boards: these promote the collective action of businesses with other private sector actors (particularly finance institutions) and, usually, government bodies. A particular group of these are Private Industry Councils (PICs).

e Enterprise Agencies: government-led vehicles which stimulate collective action between businesses and which draw in other private sector interests.

These vehicles are not mutually exclusive. The traditional forms have usually been trade associations, chambers of commerce and business clubs. These have usually had limited impact and have been dominated by narrow interests which are rarely geared to economic development, but their role is now rapidly expanding. Of greater significance have been community business schemes, such as Community Development Partnerships, Business in the Community, PICs and Enterprise Boards and Agencies. These vehicles involve business with the wider group of actors who are important in providing the conditions for success of economic development: notably, financial institutions and sources of venture capital, provision of management expertise, and support from local government and voluntary organisations. In the USA, PICs have now become an important form of such agencies, and the PIC model is being actively considered by the government in Britain. Frequently the term 'partnership' is used to denote such arrangements. This reflects the emphasis on the need to combine individual actions in order to ensure success.

The marked growth and success of these collective vehicles has emphasised endogenous and collaborative action. However, the schemes that have been most successful in the most difficult circumstances have usually involved the introduction of external investment funds, either from private sector financial institutions or from government. Thus, although the emphasis is endogenous and collective, external support is also often required. The extent of external support required, and its form, draws us to the wider effects of market failures and the necessary role of governments.

The case for government action is founded on the same criteria as private sector individual or collective actions providing the right circumstances for investment and economic growth. Government action is to be distinguished from collective action, however, by its scale, its form and its ability to enforce.

The traditional and technical definition of the requirements for government-provided goods (public goods) stem from a situation where there may be market failure. Public goods should normally have three characteristics, as follows: joint supply – supply to one individual or firm allows identical supply to all at no extra cost; impossibility of exclusion – supply to one prevents the good being withheld from others; and impossibility of rejection – once supplied, a good must be consumed equally by all. A pure public good possesses all three of these characteristics. Most public goods do not, but satisfy enough of each of these conditions to justify public action.

These public good characteristics lead to market failure which normally means that it is not in the interests of any one firm to supply the good, since this would allow free supply to other firms for no return. An example would be one firm bearing the cost of building a road connecting its factory on an industrial estate to a major highway, or one firm bearing the cost of expensive labour training in a highly mobile employment sector subject to high risks of 'poaching', or one firm embarking on a high level of pollution control which disadvantaged it in comparison with its competitors. However, despite the economic disincentives to the actions of individual firms, there are major benefits to all firms, or to the community as a whole, of undertaking such expenditures. A means has to be found, therefore, of encouraging all (or most) firms to provide so that the required benefits are obtained. This is akin to the 'prisoner's dilemma' in game theory, where individually rational action results in higher costs than collective action. The necessary agency to overcome this problem cannot usually be provided by voluntary collective action, as discussed above, but requires a government acting on behalf of a wider community, either locally or nationally.

There are a number of other limits to collective business action. For instance, strong local commitments are undermined by the mobility of employees, executives, skills and the location of firms. Also, uncertainty and imperfect information about weakly-perceived benefits undermine voluntary action, and it is not appropriate for a business to be 'an all-purpose institution that should right all social wrongs' . . . instead this is 'the job of the politician working in a democratic process . . . the businessman . . . should not be making essential social decisions' (Diebold, 1972, quoted in Baumol, 1975). Most of all, however, there is the free-rider problem, that competition between firms and their trading environment precludes large-scale voluntary activity, since a firm so engaged can be undercut and put out of business by other firms lacking the same degree of social responsibility.

Many economic development needs have strong public good attributes either at national, regional, or local level. This is often particularly true of large-scale local economic regeneration. For example, in an extreme case of urban dereliction the economic incentives to an individual business are not to reinvest, not to upgrade the quality of its premises, and not to invest in local labour skills. Rather, the local disincentives are so great as to encourage movement elsewhere or closure. This has been referred to as the Samaritan's dilemma by Buchanan (1975). However, a large number of businesses acting together in a run-down area, and businesses acting collectively with those other institutions which possess the ability to affect education, labour skills, crime levels, environmental quality, communications, access and infrastructure, can change the fortunes of an area and can stimulate regeneration. The leadership and resources required in this extreme case will normally far exceed the ability of non-government action, particularly if it is sought to make these changes over a reasonably short period of time.

The case for government action in local economic development arises from local public good characteristics. Indeed, many business requirements which have the highest degree of jointness, non-excludability and non-rejectability are characteristics of the community in which the business is located. Infrastructuie, transport facilities, environments, labour market characteristics, education facilities and crime levels are all goods dominated by local characteristics. Other public goods are regional or national public goods, because they spill over between localities. Examples include the general education level, the overall economic climate, monetary and fiscal incentives, and economic stability. It is possible, therefore, to define a hierarchy of economic development goods ranging from pure individual, to pure local and pure national public goods, with various mixed collective-individual goods in between. This hierarchy is a straightforward extension of the collective good concepts of Buchanan and Tullock (1969) to the case of local economic development, but with properties depending upon the form and extent of geographical externalities to each business.

Taking the case of geographical jointness, and combining it with jointness to collectives of businesses irrespective of their location, yields the simplified classification shown in Table 10.1. Among the main groups are pure public goods, pure individual goods and pure local public goods.

Pure public goods are those to which the traditional conditions apply – jointness, non-excludability and non-rejectability – with no geographical bounds within a given country. The provision of these is one of the main objectives of national economic policy. Pure individual goods are restricted in supply and demand to individual businesses. These goods should be held outside collective action except insofar as there is a collective benefit by collaborations. Pure local public goods are those which are joint within a given area, but restricted to those businesses in that locality. It is these which are the prime focus of local government economic development policy.

However, there is a wide range of goods which are partially joint, either between businesses or between areas. These form the nexus of the debate as to the most appropriate form of action – public or private – and also present the greatest difficulty in reaching the best combination of local and central government activities. The table gives a possible classification of some major goods and services which are of significance to business development.

This discussion forms the basis for a theoretical framework for evaluating the scope for local economic development policy, and is developed further by Bennett (1989) in terms of administrative policy, fiscal policy, expenditure policy, and debt policy. We now move to the resolution of our second question, namely the forms of actions that can be developed in a British context.

FORMS AND STRUCTURES OF PROJECTS IN BRITAIN

Both business collective action and local government economic development activities are growing rapidly in Britain, albeit from a very low base. These developments are exhibited in the analysis of a sample of local economic development initiatives drawn from LEDIS (Local Economic Development Information Service), a survey in which Sellgren (1987) identified a wide range of actions. A large proportion of these actions were initiatives taking a legal identity separate from their founders, as shown by Table 10.2.

Altogether, a quarter of the sample of developments took company status. This shows several things. First, the developments are often in a position to register and to trade as companies. Secondly, company status may be significant when raising finance. Thirdly, it may be inferred from the company status that, rather than being *ad hoc* responses to local economic crises, these initiatives were planned and coordinated and run along business lines, although the pursuit of profit may not have been their sole or major objective. A further 22.5 per cent of the initiatives were also registered companies but with charitable status, providing certain tax benefits for non-profit-orientated initiatives.

The remaining half of the initiatives took a variety of legal forms. Almost half of these – a quarter of the sample – were in-house initiatives of the agencies by which they had been founded. Of the rest, 9 per cent were managed by unelected councils or boards, and a further 5 per cent by elected councils or boards.

Table 10.1 Classification of local economic development collecting goods based on their degree of geographical and non-geographical jointness

	Geographical jointness		
Non-geographical jointness	*Fully-joint*	*Partially-joint (geographically restricted)*	*Non-joint (geographically localised)*
Fully-joint (*unrestricted between businesses*)	*Pure public goods* • General economic climate • Monetary system • National defence • Legal system • Safety standards • General fiscal incentives	• Education policy • Pollution control • Street lighting • Fire service • Police service • Markets	*Pure local public goods* • Network services electricity, gas, water, sewerage • Physical environment • Social and economic environment

Partially-joint (partially restricted between businesses)	• Postal service • Telephone and communications • Labour market character • Debt policy	• Local fiscal and expenditure policy • Roads and transport • Crime and its prevention • Flood control
Non-joint (completely restricted to single businesses)		*Pure individual goods* • Management skills • R. & D. and patents • Physical stocks, assets and plant • Staff loyalty and quality • Clients and market, goodwill and knowledge

Table 10.2 shows all the types of legal constitution adopted by initiatives set up by the range of agencies, and it demonstrates the propensity for initiatives to take a legal form similar to that of the agency responsible for setting them up. For example, it is notable that 56.4 per cent of the initiatives set up by companies themselves took company status, while 19.4 per cent of initiatives created by voluntary agencies had themselves a voluntary status. In addition, it is very common for initiatives to be run as in-house activities of the agencies which set them up. This is the case for both the 15.4 per cent of initiatives run as subsidiary companies of initiating corporations, and for 47.1 per cent of the initiatives set up by local authorities. To some extent this latter figure is an over-representation, since LEDIS contains a number of examples of the work of whole economic development units, but it is clear that many of the projects with which local authorities are involved remain under their own umbrella.

Table 10.2 Legal structure adopted by initiatives broken down by initiating agency (percentages) in a UK survey

Legal structure	*Initiating agencies:* Company	*Local authority*	*Educational body*	*Central govt dept*	*Manpower Services Commission*	*Voluntary*	*Other*
Council/ Board (elected)	5.1	1.5	0.0	7.7	0.0	2.8	12.3
Council/ Board (non-elected)	2.6	7.4	0.0	23.1	0.0	11.1	14.3
Company (charitable status)	15.4	11.8	0.0	7.7	0.0	44.4	36.7
Company	41.0	23.5	10.0	23.1	25.0	16.7	24.5
Subsidiary Company	15.4	0.0	0.0	0.0	0.0	0.0	0.0
Cooperative	7.7	0.0	0.0	0.0	0.0	2.8	2.0
Voluntary	5.1	2.9	20.0	0.0	0.0	19.4	6.1
Other	2.6	5.9	70.0	38.5	75.0	2.8	4.1
Local authority	5.1	47.1	0.0	0.0	0.0	0.0	0.0
Total	100.0	100.0	100.0	100.0	100.0	100.0	100.0

Source: Sellgren, 1987

The 'other' legal status section encompasses a number of the in-house activities of educational bodies and central government departments. Seventy per cent of initiatives set up by educational bodies remain in-house, this being largely due to the type of services provided, normally being business support schemes which form an extension to the educational facilities of the institution.

The corporate sector has been very important in setting up local economic initiatives. However, it is argued by Mason (1987) that the level of corporate involvement in collaborative projects has often been somewhat limited, and in many cases this has led to corporations developing an individualistic approach to such initiatives. It is suggested that this has arisen for two reasons: first, there may be a lack of suitable partners with which to develop projects; secondly there may be a desire on the part of some companies to act unilaterally in order to maintain control over the funds which they have allocated and also to maintain operational freedom. It is also pointed out that, in acting unilaterally, a company is able to gain maximum visibility for its efforts, although this will also apply where projects are less successful. Despite this, however, over 30 per cent of the initiatives in the LEDIS sample were supported financially by companies (Sellgren, 1987) and many companies provide considerable in-kind support through the various means discussed above.

The importance of local authorities in setting up such local economic development initiatives can be seen from the above. It was found by Sellgren (1987) that almost a third of the initiatives in the LEDIS sample were set up by a local authority. It has been argued that involvement with economic initiatives is one way in which local authorities have sought to develop their local economic development activities. Their very close involvement in such schemes therefore merits closer examination. A survey of local authorities' involvement in industrial development and economic management was undertaken in 1987 (Sellgren, 1988). The results of this survey provided detailed information on the work of over 400 individual initiatives being supported in the 1986–87 financial year. Table 10.3 shows the legal status of the local authority initiatives identified by this survey. Over 60 per cent of the initiatives which were surveyed were under the direct control of the local authority. Thus it appears that there is a strong tendency for local authorities to maintain control of economic initiatives which they set up, and this must cast some doubt on the theory that initiatives are necessarily set up at arm's length as a means of circumventing statutory limitations on local authority activities. Indeed, the fact that such a large proportion of initiatives remain under direct local authority control may reflect a rejection of arm's-length approaches, and a desire to maintain control over projects set up, managed by, or supported by the authority.

Table 10.3 Legal structure of local authority initiatives in a UK survey

Legal structure	%
Council/Board (elected)	2.2
Council/Board (non-elected)	0.2
Company (charitable status)	4.4
Company (status not stated)	12.1
Company	5.1
In-house to another initiative	0.2
Cooperative	0.7
Voluntary	1.2
Local authority	61.7
Local authority and government department	2.7
Local authority and private sector	4.6
Manpower Services Commission (MSC)	1.0
Educational body	0.2
Trust	1.9
Management agreement	0.2
Other	1.5

Source: Sellgren (1988)

The remaining 177 initiatives were structured under a variety of legal forms, reflecting a similar range to those identified by the LEDIS sample. As with the LEDIS analysis, initiatives which had company status were well represented, with 21.6 per cent of those analysed having some form of company status. Perhaps not surprisingly, however, none of the initiatives identified in this survey were run as subsidiary companies. Examples of these were found in the LEDIS analysis, where large companies had set up subsidiary operations to assist economic development.

In the LEDIS analysis 14.1 per cent of initiatives were constituted and run by councils and boards. The incidence of these in the local authority survey was very much lower, with only 2.4 per cent of initiatives being organised in this manner. The survey of local authority involvement with economic initiatives identified a small but significant number of cooperative ventures (0.7 per cent) and also a number (1.2 per cent) being run on a voluntary basis. The survey also identified a few schemes (1.9 per cent) which had trust status. Since the LEDIS analysis had identified a series of linkages –

particularly financial – between local and national government in the operation of local initiatives, it may have been considered a priori that local authorities would be involved with initiatives for which government departments or agencies were primarily responsible. However, the results of the local authority survey showed a very low level of such involvement, with no authorities being involved with government projects and only a few examples of collaboration in schemes run by the Manpower Services Commission (1 per cent). However, 2.7 per cent of the schemes had been developed through local and central government partnerships. The survey also identified a significant number of schemes (4.6 per cent) which were operated as partnerships between the local authorities and the private sector. It has already been suggested that initiatives are characterised by the collaborative nature of their operation, so it is not surprising to find schemes which are set up with a collaborative partnership status.

The LEDIS analysis found that almost 80 per cent of the initiatives were associated with some form of advisory facility. The survey of local authority economic initiatives found the largest category of activities to be those concerned with business support (35.6 per cent). Perhaps the best-known business support projects are Enterprise Agencies and Enterprise Trusts (see, for example, Deloitte, Haskins and Sells, 1984, and McCreadie, 1985). Local authorities play an important role in sponsoring Enterprise Agencies: in 1987 they accounted for 11.6 per cent of the total number of agency sponsors. Table 10.4 shows the level of local authority sponsorship to individual Enterprise Agencies

Table 10.4 Level of local authority sponsorship to UK Enterprise Agencies

Percentage of agencies supported by:		
0	county (regional) councils	55.7
1	county (regional) councils	43.3
2	county (regional) councils	1.0
Percentage of agencies supported by:		
0	district (borough) councils	17.9
1	district (borough) councils	57.8
2	district (borough) councils	11.3
3	district (borough) councils	6.2
4	district (borough) councils	4.1
5	district (borough) councils	1.4
6	district (borough) councils	1.0
7	district (borough) councils	0.0
8	district (borough) councils	0.3

Source: Business in the Community: *Directory of Enterprise Agencies*, 1986, 1987

in 1987. It is clear that more than half of all Enterprise Agencies tend to be supported at least by their local district (or borough) councils, and that a considerable number will also be supported by the county (or regional) authority. In some measure the number of authorities sponsoring an agency will be indicative of the catchment area covered by the individual Agency. The principal activity common to all Enterprise Agencies is the provision of free advice and counselling support for the setting-up and development of viable small business. In addition to this, a large proportion of Agencies have begun to develop a wider range of services to complement the advisory role. These services include the provision of managed workshops, training courses for organisational skills, and the provision of loans and grant funds. Enterprise Agencies are often, but not always, companies limited by guarantee.

Table 10.5 shows the principal activities of Enterprise Agencies in 1986 and 1987. The figures are based on the 245 Enterprise Agencies listed in 1986 and the 282 listed in 1987. The central importance of counselling services is illustrated very clearly: this activity is the cornerstone of the Enterprise Agencies' activities. In discussing the role of Glasgow Opportunities (one of the Glasgow Agencies) Paterson (1985) argues that the one-stop-shop approach to providing free and confidential advice in a non-bureaucratic manner

Table 10.5 Activities of UK Enterprise Agencies, 1986, 1987

	1986	*1987*
	%	%
Counselling	100.0	100.0
Training courses/seminars	41.2	79.4
Exhibitions	35.1	59.2
Newsletters	35.1	51.8
Educational liaison schemes	37.1	69.1
Small business club	29.0	46.1
Access to loan/grant funds	31.8	58.6
Property register	25.3	39.7
Meet the buyer	19.2	22.0
Trade directory	20.8	30.1
Workspaces	22.0	46.1
Business-to-business	13.9	20.2
Business competition	16.3	19.1
Youth enterprise	19.2	43.6
Resource-matching bureau	9.4	14.9

Source: Business in the Community: *Directory of Enterprise Agencies*, 1986, 1987

has proved to be the model for most Enterprise Agencies in the country. In addition, it is suggested that the Agencies' own business contacts have been an important factor in their performance. It has been pointed out, for example, by Deloitte, Haskins and Sells (1984), that in providing a counselling service an Enterprise Agency does not necessarily have to possess a large full-time staff. Indeed, a recent BiC (undated) survey found 90 per cent of Agencies surveyed had five or fewer full-time staff, with an average per agency being 3.2 full-timers and 2 part-timers. Many Agencies have developed extensive networks of contacts to whom they may direct a client for specialist advice or support. These may be drawn from the Agencies' sponsors, central and local government, development agencies, or financial and educational institutions.

It is evident that Enterprise Agencies appear to have increasingly supported their counselling activities through other services, notably through training courses and seminars. In addition, however, activities such as producing newsletters and organising business clubs have been offered by an increasing proportion of Agencies. It is also notable that significant numbers of Agencies are active in assisting firms in respect of land and premises, either indirectly through the production of property registers, or directly through the provision or management of workspaces. Increasing direct financial involvement with firms to which Enterprise Agencies have offered their services is evident in the growing availability of loan and grant funds by almost 60 per cent of Agencies in 1987. It is also apparent that Enterprise Agencies have sought to involve themselves increasingly with potential entrepreneurs of the future through seeking to assist youth enterprise and also by educational liaison schemes.

In seeking to ascertain the contribution of Enterprise Agencies to small firm survival and job creation, a report by Enterprise Dynamics for Business in the Community (BiC, undated) was able to be quite positive about the performance of the Agencies which they had studied. It was found that businesses assisted by Enterprise Agencies had a superior survival rate when compared with other small firms – for example those assisted under the Enterprise Allowance Scheme – since it was noted that the failure rate was of the order of 1 in 6, compared with a national figure of 1 in 3. It was also found that firms assisted by Enterprise Agencies appeared to be contributing to job creation. A sample of 285 surviving firms which had been assisted showed that they had an average net gain of one job per business in the previous twelve-month period. In terms of the facilities and services offered by Enterprise Agencies, it was found that general and start-up advice was rated as the single most valuable form of Agency assistance by 43 per cent of the surviving firms surveyed. Where Agencies offered workshop facilities, these ranked third behind general information and financial advice. A study carried out by the Centre for Employment Initiatives on behalf of the Community Initiatives Research Trust (Centre for Employment Initiatives, 1985) took a random sample of Enterprise Agency clients and found that 10 per cent of respondents would not have started in business without the involvement of the Agency, or felt that their enterprise would have folded. A further 44 per cent stated that without the Agency it would have taken longer for them to have achieved what they had achieved or that they would have found it more difficult. Finally, 45 per cent of respondents felt that the assistance which they had from the Agency did not have an effect on what they had done. This survey also asked the clients to make an assessment of the Agency's role in helping to create or save jobs (within their own enterprises). The results found that 19 per cent of respondents felt that the help they had received from the Agency was crucial, 38 per cent rated the Agency's help as useful, 14 per cent felt the Agency's help had been marginal, and 29 per cent of respondents regarded the Agency's role as irrelevant in helping to create or save jobs.

CONCLUSIONS: FUTURE POSSIBILITIES FOR COLLECTIVE ACTION

We have argued that businesses have an interest in local economic development, internal and external to their firms both from the perspective of their own 'self-interest', altruism and social responsibility, and also from wider social goals. However, it is clear that there are very definite limits to voluntary collective action; these arise from the need for firms to remain competitive and to prevent themselves being undercut by non-altruistic free-riders. Thus it has been argued that a level of government action is required which sets, for all firms, a comparable local framework for social or collective action. Such a framework is subject to severe constraints. Compliance costs of government action must be minimised as well as offering minimum distortions to factor combinations and economic efficiency. Government regulatory policy, therefore, provides only limited scope for extending the range of business collective action. This leads to the introduction of the need for government action to take on a level of public service provision.

We have argued that the best level of government action relates to expenditure policy, chiefly through selective advisory services and general local public goods, but also through facilitative and regulatory administrative policy. Public choice theory has been used to define a possible classification of public good activities of central and local government. A classification of localised 'jointness' of activities is critical to defining the economic development needs of localities. It is suggested that, in the most difficult situations requiring substantial economic regeneration, only the central government can play the most effective role, but local government in conjunction with the private sector and private institutions can also be effective. There is arguably a legitimate interest in restricting pure promotion and advertising activities by localities since these are deadweight burdens with zero-sum outcomes. Beyond such activities, however, local government policies can be most effective if linked with the appropriate management skills and understanding provided by businesses. Although businesses have limited expertise, time and resources to understand and act on issues of 'social responsibility', in most countries, but particularly in Britain, more support for these activities could be made than is the case at present. The model of Enterprise Agencies may be particularly useful in this context, since it suggests a means of not only providing cost-effective support, but also overcoming business suspicions. This suggests that the prime emphasis should be on partnership approaches to local economic developments. And this draws us to our conclusion on the most appropriate policy instruments.

Facilitative and supportive actions by government, business social responsibility and Enterprise Agencies suggest that the primary instruments should be providing counselling and advice, particularly in start-up and expansion of small businesses, and providing limited financial support, particularly equity. The latter instrument requires, in turn, widening the access to risk and venture capital. Other important instruments include widening the supportive environment of local and other actors (including government), particularly by the use of pump-priming, and other broad support, which seeks to get the local pre-conditions right. In this context, the central government's role, because of its larger and broader-based resources, is likely to be most important.

The current debate focuses on two aspects of local government powers: first, the role of the Section 137 powers of the 1972 Local Government Act, and secondly, the most appropriate legal framework for local authority involvement in companies. At present the activities of local government in Britain are circumscribed by the *ultra vires* doctrine which has been developed to ensure that public authorities act only in an authorised manner bound by the rule of law. Even where statutory authorisation is available, it is still possible for a decision to be declared *ultra vires* where the local authority has contravened some principle of common law. Thus authorities may exceed their powers in a manner which the courts maintain Parliament did not intend. Economic development is an activity for which local authorities have no specific powers. However, they may undertake such activity under a variety of statutory powers. A study by JURUE (1980) classified four types of power that may be used for economic development activity:

a statutory duties for employment services;
b statutory duties for other services which are not primarily concerned with employment objectives but may have an incidental effect upon them;
c permissive powers given to local authorities which may be used in certain circumstances to undertake employment initiatives; and
d local powers arising either from Local Acts or from Special Acts which apply only to some local authorities or within specified areas.

In addition to the statutory provisions, local authorities are able to draw upon their common law powers to do anything which is reasonably incidental to their statutory functions.

Local authorities also have permissive powers which allow them, if they wish, to undertake a variety of additional activities. The most important of these powers are Sections 2, 3 and 4 of the Local Authorities (Land) Act 1963 which enable authorities to undertake or support the provision of land, buildings and infrastructure and to provide advance factories, warehouses or small units. Under the Local Authority Superannuation Regulations of 1974 and 1984, authorities are empowered to invest up to 10 per cent of their superannuation funds in unquoted securities, and this may include local firms. The Local Government Act 1972 and Local Government (Scotland) Act 1973, provide a variety of powers which local authorities may be able to utilise for economic development work and these include appointing staff (Section 112/64): thus local authorities can appoint people to industrial development posts, and they can arrange lectures, hold discussions or mount displays on matters relating to local government (Section 142/88). Further, local authorities can engage in a variety of activities to collect, publish and circulate information relating to their areas and thus to promote them. Sections 111/69 of these Acts make a general provision which empowers local authorities to do anything conducive or incidental to the discharge of any of their functions, and this may include setting up economic or industrial development units. Local authorities are also empowered to engage in some limited municipal enterprises: these include the establishment and maintenance of municipal restaurants, markets and slaughterhouses, and also the provision of a varied range of goods and services which may be used by other local authorities or public bodies.

The most widely publicised permissive power which may be used to undertake economic development is Section 137 of the Local Government Act 1972 for England and Wales, and its equivalent Section 83 of the Local Government (Scotland) Act 1973. Under these provisions, local authorities have been able to incur expenditure in the interest of their area or its inhabitants, up to a maximum of a 2p product of the rates. However, this power has been reviewed on a number of occasions, most recently by the Widdicombe Committee (Widdicombe, 1986). This concluded that the existing position relating to Section 137/83 could be clarified by maintaining the notion of ensuring that benefits accrue to the local area, but 'defining more precisely the degree of benefits which must be achieved' (Widdicombe, 1986, paragraph 8.85). They also felt that the yield from any discretionary power needed to be regulated. The most important recommendations were as follows:

a that local authorities should have a financially limited discretionary power to spend in the interests of their area;
b that there should be a review of the proper role of local authorities in economic development, taking account of the role of other governmental agencies, with a view to identifying any area in which additional local authority statutory powers should be introduced – this review should include enterprise boards and arm's-length companies;
c that the expenditure limit under Section 137/83 should be set in future in relation to the population of an area;
d that this limit should be regularly reviewed, by Order;
e that the limit be set at £5 per head of population;
f that the limit for single-tier authorities should be double that applying to two-tier authorities;
g that the 2p limit for expenditure under Section 137/83 be increased to 4p as an interim measure before a population base is introduced;
h that Section 137 for England and Wales be amended to be comparable to Section 83 for Scotland, such that a local authority may use its power for a purpose for which another local authority

has statutory responsibility only with the consent of that other local authority; and

i that the law concerning local authority controlled companies should be amended to make clear that they may be set up only where there is specific enabling legislation and to incorporate safeguards on articles of association, membership, audit and reporting.

The main government response to these proposals is contained in a white paper (HMSO, 1988a). In this they argued that, whilst affirming that authorities should continue to exercise a general power of discretion to spend in the interests of their area, the government should seek to limit this financially and should legislate for a new specific power outside Sections 137/83 for the case of local economic development policy. The new financial limit has been set at £5 per head of adult population (divided into £2.50 each for two-tier authorities), but with no interim increase in financial powers. The effect of the new limit, in comparison with the previous 2p rate product, varies between areas, depending on the relationship between population size and rateable value. Whilst significant, the increase does not keep up with the value of the 2p rate product defined originally in 1972.

On the question of local authority companies, a decision by the government will depend upon its response to a consultation paper issued in June 1988 (HMSO, 1988b). However, the shape of the government's position is already clear. First, they reject the Widdicombe Committee's recommendation (see point i above) that local authority controlled companies should be set up only where there is specific enabling legislation. The government propose, instead, that local authorities should have a controlling interest in only those companies whose activities are within the local authorities' powers and duties, and that a minority interest can be held only in specific circumstances. They define permitted classes of minority interest to include:

a public transport companies;
b public airport companies;
c companies related to further education;
d housing associations;
e Enterprise Agencies;
f management companies of land, buildings and structures;
g land development companies;
h statutory companies; and
i professional associations.

Within these constraints, the government proposes to follow the Widdicombe Committee recommendation that safeguards be incorporated into the ways in which companies are run. They consider it to be an anomaly that local authorities' interests in companies are outside the rules which govern the conduct, scope and financial procedures and propriety of local authority businesses. In particular, the government seeks to ensure that a local authority company should not do anything that the controlling authority could not do; in other words, it does not want a local authority company to act *ultra vires*, except in the provision of services between the authority and its company, or under the Transport Act, or in preparation for privatisation. Thus the government has sought to stop local authorities circumventing restrictions on their powers, particularly restrictions on their capital accounts imposed by central government and restrictions on membership which apply to local authorities but which have not affected companies.

As a result, the capital transactions of local authority controlled companies are to be brought within the framework applying to local authorities generally. There are to be new requirements for the presentation of accounts and audit. Statutory rules are to be imposed on personnel involved. There is to be a code of practice and there is to be a prohibition on local authorities holding interests in companies outside the EC. Politically most significant is the bringing of local authority companies within the net of capital controls and the restrictions on personnel.

It is clear from these developments that the Government has accepted a role for local government control of companies, but only within very specific guidelines related to economic development and underpinning private sector interest. This seems to be closely in line with the theoretical conclusions of this paper.

REFERENCES

Baumol, W.J. (1975) 'Business responsibility and economic behavior', in E.S. Phelps (ed.) *Altruism, Morality and Economic Theory*, pp. 45–56, New York: Russell Sage Foundation.

Bennett, R.J. (1989) 'Local economic development: the possibilities and the limitations of decentralised policy', in R.J. Bennett (ed.) *Decentralisation: Setting the New Intergovernmental Agendas*, Oxford: Oxford University Press.

BiC (1986) *Business and the Inner City*, London: Business in the Community.

BiC (undated) *Small Firms: Survival and Job Creation: the Contribution of Enterprise Agencies*, London: Business in the Community.

Buchanan, J.M. (1965) 'An economic theory of clubs' *Economica* 32:1.
Buchanan, J.M. (1971) 'Principles of urban fiscal strategy', *Public Choice* 11:1.
Buchanan, J.M. (1975) 'The Samaritan's dilemma', in E.S. Phelps (ed.) *Altruism, Morality and Economic Theory*, pp. 71–85, New York: Russell Sage Foundation.
Buchanan, J.M. and Tullock, G. (1969) *The Calculus of Consent*, Ann Arbor: University of Michigan Press.
Centre for Employment Initiatives (1985) *The Impact of Local Enterprise Agencies in Great Britain: Operational Lessons and Policy Implications*, London: CEI/BiC.
Deloitte, Haskins & Sells (1984) *Local Enterprise Agencies: a New and Growing Feature of the Economy*, London: Deloitte, Haskins & Sells.
Davies, R. (1988) 'Approaches from the private sector', in R.J. Bennett and W. Plowden (eds) *Local Economic Development: Identifying the Research Priorities*, pp. 40–42, London: Economic and Social Research Council.
Diebold, J. (1972) *The Social Responsibility of Business*, (conference address), cited in W.J. Baumol (1975) pp. 46–7.
HMSO (1988a) *The Conduct of Local Authority Business: the Government Response to the Report of the Widdicombe Committee of Inquiry*, Cmnd 433, London.
HMSO (1988b) *Local Authorities' Interest in Companies: A Consultation Paper*, London: Department of the Environment.
JURUE (1980) *Local Authority Employment Initiatives*, Birmingham: Joint Unit for Research on the Urban Environment.
Mason, C. (1987) 'Job creation initiatives in the UK: the large company role', *Industrial Relations Journal*, 18:4.
McCreadie, J. (ed.) (1985) 'Enterprise agencies and local economic development', *Planning Exchange: Occasional Paper No.17*, Planning Exchange, Glasgow.
Paterson, G. 'Developing counselling and advisory services', in J. McCreadie (ed.).
Sellgren, J. (1987) 'Local economic development and local initiatives in the mid-1980s: an analysis of the Local Economic Development Information Service', *Local Government Studies* 13:6.
Sellgren, J. (1988) 'Assisting local economies: an assessment of emerging patterns of local authority economic development activities', in D.C. Gibbs (ed.) *Government Policy and Industrial Change*, London: Routledge.
Widdicombe, D. (1986) *The Conduct of Local Authority Business: Report of the Committee of Enquiry into the Conduct of Local Authority Business*, 1985–6, Cmnd 9797, Chaired by Mr David Widdicombe QC, London: HMSO.

Index

Page numbers in italic refer to figures or tables.